St[...]g

our Land

The Law, Rent & Taxation

Kenneth Jupp

Published by
VINDEX
in association with the
LAND POLICY COUNCIL

First published in 1997 by
Vindex
in association with the
Land Policy Council,
London

VINDEX
is an imprint of
Othila Press Ltd.,
58a Abingdon Road,
London, W8 6AP, UK

British Library CIP Data
A catalogue record of this book
is available from the British Library

ISBN 1 901647 00 5

Printed in Great Britain by
MFP Design & Print,
Manchester

Contents

PART I

The Decline of Justice

1

The Fount of Law

Throughout Christian history until comparatively modern times, it was believed that mankind lived under a universal moral law, known by reason and confirmed by revelation, objective and unchanging, binding upon them in spite of their failure to observe it. Thus at the beginning of the 17th century Chief Justice Coke was able to say in Bonham's case[1]:

> When an Act of Parliament is against common right and reason, the common law will control it, and adjudge such Act to be void.

Similarly, in the middle of the 18th century the celebrated jurist Blackstone, in his *Analysis of the Laws of England*,[2] wrote:

(1) Law is a Rule of Action prescribed by a superior power.

(2) Natural Law is the Rule of Human action, prescribed by the Creator, and discoverable by the Light of Reason.

(3) The Divine, or Revealed, Law (considered as a Rule of Action) is also the Law of Nature, imparted by God himself.

This was still the orthodox teaching of the Church as

expounded by Thomas Aquinas. It is only during the last hundred years or so that the idea of Natural Law has fallen into disfavour and Divine Law has been forgotten. During that time politicians and lawyers came more and more to accept the power of the modern state as absolute, and concentrated on the elaboration of "positive law", as they call it, rather than on its ideological basis. This trend can easily be recognised in the laws emanating from the European Community. When these laws do not fit the facts in the locality where they have to be applied, they give rise to deep feelings of injustice. Legislators remote from the scene rarely have the experience to know what is needed in practice.

Natural Law and Natural Justice are now entirely out of fashion. The whole trend of philosophy has for long been against such concepts. It is taken for granted that government is under no higher law - that so long as those currently in power keep strictly to the rules of procedure in legislating, their fiat cannot be challenged, however unreasonable it may be. *Ultra vires* has almost entirely come to mean not in accordance with the powers conferred by statute. The word 'law' has thus come to mean little more than 'the will of the powerful'. Even the courts now regard statute law as overriding common law absolutely. In effect, our judges are there to implement the will of those in power in Westminster, or in appropriate cases, in Brussels. This is the principle of Roman Law underlying the legal systems of continental Europe, namely, *Quod principi placet legis habet valorem* - what pleases the prince (i.e. the government) has the force of law. The English Common Law by contrast harks back to the thirteenth century Justiciar, Bracton, who declared:

> The king must not be under any man but under God and under the law, because law made the king;

to which Lord Denning in recent times has added:

> To every subject in this land, no matter how powerful, I would use Thomas Fuller's words over 300 years ago. 'Be you never so high the law is above you'.[3]

This may have been wishful thinking. We talk of democracy. But we live under an oligarchy of legislators and administrators who are called to order periodically at election time, when the people are offered a choice of the same or a different oligarchy with but slightly different aims, to rule unrestrained by traditional laws and customs. Only a very few have any idea of an overriding natural law, much less a supreme divine law: and these few have little or no influence. At best our system of government could be called democratic tyranny.

The Church and the Scriptures

Even more remarkable is the inability of the Christian Church to guide the politicians, economists, teachers and others who mould and influence public opinion, by appealing to scripture in search of the divine law from which natural law could be deduced. When Church leaders descend into the realm of politics and economics today it is often either to take sides between the political parties, or to urge that more government funds be made available for inner city development or the like. In April 1997, for example, in anticipation of the general election, the Council of Churches published a report on unemployment which highlighted the shocking prevalence of poverty and unemployment in Britain. This was very welcome, indeed overdue. They point out that with poverty comes social exclusion and despair, but they do not refer to Christ's having said exactly that in Mt. 5; 3. They refer to 9.8 million people dependent on income support as being intolerable, as indeed it is. They conclude that the only satisfactory solution is to reduce the numbers dependent on benefit. They are right. The remedy is to get rid of poverty instead of supporting poverty by trying to relieve it. This needed saying, and one can only hope their message will be learnt. But when the report suggested remedies, there was no reference to the remedy taught by Christ. Instead the report took refuge in the outworn doctrines of economics - a dismal and atheistic science - by recommending many of its failed nostrums: higher taxation, and public spending (on jobs 'created' at the taxpayer's expense), a national minimum wage, workers' rights, and even a subsidy for employers taking on the long term unemployed. Yet the founder of the Christian faith had much to say on the subject of the poor, the meek, and the oppressed, and how by observance of the Torah (the divine law) they would be liberated from their plight. Those who heard him at the time rejected his teaching and attempted to kill him. That teaching is scarcely to be heard today; although faint glimmerings of it appear in South American 'liberation theology'.[4]

The scriptures make it clear that the land is our inheritance; that the inheritance has to be shared; and that the law has to sustain this position, and by constant review and updating, prevent it from degenerating because of changing circumstances into wealth and poverty existing side by side - Dives with Lazarus at his gate[5].

To become free the children of Israel working under hard task masters in Egypt had to have a land of their own. So God promised them the Holy Land. This had to be obtained by conquest, and Joshua was ordered to conquer Canaan. But the land belongs only to God, and after conquest must be divided fairly between all families that constitute the nation:

> The Lord said to Moses: "... Ye shall dispossess the inhabitants of the land, and dwell therein: for I have given you the land to possess it. And ye shall divide the land by lot for an inheritance among your families: and to the more ye shall give the more inheritance, and to the fewer ye shall give the less inheritance. (Numbers 33: 53 - 54. Similarly in Num. 26: 55, 56).
>
> The Lord said to Joshua: "All the inhabitants [of the land that yet remaineth] ... will I drive out from before the children of Israel: only divide thou it by lot unto the Israelites for an inheritance, as I have commanded thee." (Joshua 13: 6).

The Torah also ensured that families would never lose their right to land. It therefore ordained periodical review and reinstatement to prevent the land falling into the hands of those who can thereby enrich themselves and oppress the poor, with the result that the rich man clothed in fine linen and faring sumptuously has Lazarus laid at his gate full of sores, seeking to be fed on the crumbs which fell from the rich man's table (Lk. 16: 19-21). Jesus in the

7

synagogue at Nazareth[6] preached "the gospel to the poor ... the acceptable year of the Lord". This was the jubilee year which the Torah enjoined as the means of preserving the equitable division of land. In the jubilee year, all debts were to be cancelled; all debtors who had been enslaved for default in payment had to be released; and all land taken as security, or otherwise bought or sold had to revert to the families whose inheritance it was.

The Christian Church is silent upon this teaching. Yet this description of how land is obtained, and how it should be dealt with fits what has happened the world over, including our own experience in the invasions of Celt, Saxon, Dane, Viking, and Norman. Land is sometimes obtained by discovery of empty regions, but almost always by conquest in greater or less degree. That it has to be divided fairly is understood as Natural Law by aboriginal peoples. But the more separated they become from Nature, the more they forget the justice of land-division. When religion declines in modern society, Mammon is worshipped not least in the speculative buying and selling of the nation's inheritance. Those who have lost their inheritance perish unless looked after, as they ultimately are in European countries, by charity or the state. This degrading dependency on state support is no proper substitute for being given the opportunity to support their families by their own honest labour.

The Seeds of Revolution

Bernard Shaw begins his *Revolutionist's Handbook* with a quotation from Sir Robert Giffen's *Essays in Finance:*

No-one can contemplate the present condition of the masses of the people without desiring something like a revolution.[7]

Sir Robert was Assistant Editor of the *Economist* from 1868 to 1876. His observation is relevant to the world today. The parlous condition of Third World countries, usually desperately poor, and often oppressed by tyrannical and corrupt government, is obvious enough. Russia, ravaged by war, has been ruined by seventy years of Marxist socialism shaped by Stalin's tyrannical rule. In the United States of America - perhaps the richest country in the world - the media have portrayed slum-districts plagued by crime, drug abuse, and street violence. The ghettos of the poor blacks have been seen close to on our television screens. The absurdities of race relations meant to help the ex-slave population is beginning to be seen as doing injustice through positive discrimination against whites. In the developed countries of the world, the remarkable advances in science and technology have led to wealthy billionaires living alongside poverty relieved by welfare expenditure on such a scale that the taxpayer cannot meet its cost. Governments in consequence are compelled to borrow to an extent that endangers the economy by setting up inflation.

This would seem to justify Shaw's desire for revolution. AND YET (his capitals):

Revolutions never lightened the burden of tyranny: they have only shifted it to another shoulder.[8]

And the reason? Shaw cites Hegel's well-known pronouncement on the Philosophy of History:

What experience and history teach is this - that people and governments never have learnt from history, or acted on principles deduced from it.

This despondent conclusion is certainly brought out by the history of public finance over the last nine or ten centuries which is the subject of this book. But the proper deduction from it is that although we do not learn from history, it is only because of our ignorance of history. Most people are interested in the past. They like to know about their forebears; about the place where they live; about the country, or county, or town from which their family hailed. Family trees are made. Old Bibles which record all the weddings and funerals are carefully preserved. The Public Record Office is crowded during the lunch-time break. But comparatively few look at the origins and growth of the nation and its institutions: at the contributions made to it by Celt, Roman, Saxon, Dane, Viking, Norman, and others. Moreover for some time now the tendency in our schools and universities has been for education in history to be limited to the recent past. As a result, a whole generation now knows very little about the origins of Britain, its people, and its institutions. The result is that argument on important issues is frequently ill-informed through lack of long-term historical perspective.

We believe that history, if only it is taken back far enough, can be of great assistance in righting the wrongs from which we are suffering today. There is no need for revolution. What is needed is enlightenment as to how our troubles originated, resulting in an informed desire to change them. It is the desire without the knowledge that is so dangerous to society. We need to know the origin of the ills we wish to cure. A proper and more optimistic view of the value of history is one expressed in *Chambers' Encyclopaedia.*[9]

> It seems logical to assume that if political action is to be successful it must be based on the complete understanding of a given situation, and nothing can be understood without a knowledge of how it came to be. On the analogy between the human organism and organic society, it is assumed that to cure the diseases of society, it is necessary to know its case history.

The unwholesome state of affairs we are concerned with is, of course, to be found worldwide. But it is more easily dealt with by confining our attention to the history of one country. Nevertheless, reference to other cultures at other times and in other places will, *mutatis mutandis,* demonstrate a remarkable similarity to our island story.

The Burden of Taxation

Society today is sick: in body, mind and spirit. In Britain as in other rich nations there is a huge burden of taxation, and of public and private debt. Yet there is constant pressure from all quarters for more public money to fund all manner of causes, worthy and unworthy. The economy is under constant strain. Law-abiding people, laden with debt, devote a large proportion of what is left of their earnings after tax to servicing mortgage of their houses, and hire-purchase or leasing of their more valuable possessions such as cars, furniture, etc. These arrangements result in ownership of their houses and some of their possessions being vested in bankers and financiers, while the addition of interest to the purchase price makes them pay for things twice. Financiers grow rich on high interest rates; while their customers remain poor.

The purpose of this enquiry is to discover how this extraordinary state of affairs came about: how the economy came to be so distorted; how taxation in peacetime came into being; and how it grew to its present high level. Why over the last three centuries or so, have the remarkable advances in science and technology, which should have increased the prosperity of all, impoverished many, and considerably widened the gap between the rich and the poor to such an extent as to inflame class hatred? How is it possible for a £1m Christmas bonus to be announced for some workers in Lombard Street, while an agricultural worker is fortunate if he gets a bonus in hundreds of pounds?

Behind the strictly financial history with which we shall be dealing lies the political history of wars, rebellions and treachery. One can read of these with feelings of excitement, and at times with pride. But the social history of dire poverty - a catalogue of cruelty, injustice, and suffering - can only make one shudder.

Jane Austen, at the very beginning of the nineteenth century, introduces us to a wonderful world where nothing was known of slums, workhouses, prisons, convicts held in hulks on the Thames to await transportation or hanging; nothing of flogging or press gangs (although two of her brothers were naval officers), and much else of the social history of her time. Yet transportation went on until the middle of the nineteenth century. In 1790, when Jane was fifteen years old, Captain Arthur Phillip, the first Governor of New South Wales, was reporting that out of 930 male convicts sent out to his penal settlement, 311 had died on the journey, and 450 were sick, many of them hopelessly so. Many who were physically capable were incurably idle.[10] In 1810, the year before her first novel was published, the Archbishop of Canterbury, the Bishop of London, and five other bishops voted with a majority in the House of Lords to throw out the repeal of a statute which made stealing five shillings from a shop a capital offence.[11] One is naturally moved to ask: Who is to blame for this state of affairs? And how could it go unnoticed by so many people? The story is a long one, and the answer has to be found in developments which have taken place over nearly ten centuries.

Up until the early Middle Ages, under the feudal system, land paid all the costs of government. Feudalism has come to carry connotations of privilege on the one hand and oppression on the other. Indeed it was a system of unequal hereditary status. Yet it stood for a kind of rough justice, where no one was so high that his privileges were not conditional upon the discharge of obligations, and no one was so low that he was without certain rights. Although in practice it often fell short of this ideal, it was only when feudalism began to disintegrate that privilege became wholly divorced from obligation, and rights went by the board. This disintegration was inextricably tied to the increasing treatment of land as unconditionally owned private property (in fact, but *not* in law), and of the increasing dependence of government upon other sources for its revenue. Who, then, can be blamed?

The kings? Yes. From the Norman conquest onwards the dynastic pride and avarice of the kings led them constantly to seek additions to their landed possessions, and their wars impoverished the nation. Richard I, Edward I, Edward III, fought glorious wars, which brought nothing about. The large areas of land they had so successfully fought for were all lost. Richard, an absentee King, burdened the nation with his outrageously high ransom, raised in part through a subsidy which all had to pay. The Edwards left hundreds of discharged soldiers unable to keep themselves once the booty and ransom money won in the wars had been used up.

One who has been chiefly blamed for the financial instability of the country which led to the signing of Magna Carta is King John. But it was not his fault that as the youngest of four sons his grandfather tellingly nicknamed him 'Lackland'. It was his misfortune to be left penniless in charge of the country while his brother won glory and popularity in expensive, useless wars, leaving John to extort money from the people to pay for it all. But John was certainly not blameless. His own wars were both costly and ineffective, and ended in a French invasion.

The Barons? Yes. They were refusing to pay proper dues for their land as tenants-in-chief, but that did not stop them from insisting on payment to them of their under-tenants' dues. Their own dues of knight service having been commuted into a money payment called scutage (shield-money), they not only forced the king in Magna

Carta at Runnymede to keep scutage at the ridiculously outdated level of John's grandfather's time, they revealed their pettiness and arrogance by refusing to observe the Concord of Runnymede.[12]

The Church? Yes. The ecclesiastical landlords were some of the richest in the land. They bore a fair share of the guilt of land enclosure which played a significant role in transforming good honest men into landless rogues and vagabonds. Their indictment was well set out in the 14th century in Langland's *Piers Plowman*. They never taught the people the true doctrine of Christ. With many pious exceptions whom Langland praises, they became rich at the expense of their flocks.

The petty gentry of the shires and the yeomen? Yes. They were among the enclosers whom the early Tudors tried to restrain with Inclosure Acts - i.e. Acts designed to *prevent* Inclosure. "The class mainly responsible was that loosely but conveniently described as the 'squirearchy'. In Leicestershire this class carried out nearly 60 per cent of the enclosures made in the years 1485-1550, and over 70 per cent of those in 1551-1607".[13]

The judges? Yes. They went along with the harsh treatment of those who were unable to get a living because they could only do so by finding a master from whom they could get wages: and all too frequently there was no such master. Many of the harsh penalties for minor offences were within the jurisdiction of the justices of the peace, who were usually local landowners. There were honourable exceptions, when in the cause of justice some judges found ways of circumventing the law by inviting juries to bring in false verdicts of acquittal.

The common people? Yes. They applauded the ruinously expensive exploits of the most popular kings, and contributed to Richard's ransom money with a good grace. When the Black Death struck in 1348, they were happy enough to move their stricken neighbour's landmark and add his land to their own. It may be that the only ones to escape censure were those who suffered most from the rapacious behaviour of so many - the very small peasant farmer who lost his land. These unholy desires could hardly have had free reign if it had not been for ignorance of the consequences of their actions. "Forgive them, Lord, for they know not what they do." Blameworthiness helps to identify the source of our collective problems, but our objective is to ask what should be done to redress the balance.

2

Natural Law & Tribal Societies

In Part III of this study we shall be setting out the kind of legislation which is needed to bring our economic system more into line with Natural Law. There are important precedents to be cited so as to ensure that the modern solution remains faithful to an anthropological history that is timeless.

As one writes about the long and slow development of England, one is struck by how similar it was, although in slow motion, to the swift development of more recently discovered countries; especially North America and Australia. This similarity was observed by Sir John Clapham in his lectures at Cambridge. He describes the early Saxon settlers as "a mobile, colonizing, frontier sort of population".[14] Trevelyan too:[15]

> In certain respects the conditions of pioneer life in the shires of Saxon England and the Danelaw were not unlike those of North America and Australia in the nineteenth century: the lumberman with his axe, the log shanty in the clearing, the draught oxen, the horses to ride to the nearest farm five miles across the wilderness, the weapon ever laid close to hand beside the axe and plough, the rough word and ready blow, and the good comradeship of the

frontiersman. And in Saxon England, as in later America, there were the larger, older, and more settled townships, constantly catching up and assimilating the pioneers who had first started human life in some 'deep den' of the woodlands. Every one of the sleepy, leisurely, garden-like villages of rural England was once a pioneer settlement, an outpost of man planted and battled for in the midst of nature's primeval realm.

One also gets a strong impression of how much nearer to Nature and to God - pagan or Christian - they lived. This is true of all tribal peoples. The American Indians, the Australian aborigines, the Maoris of New Zealand, the African Negroes, all felt their dependence on their environment of land, sea, and sky; animal and vegetable life; and the resources yielded to them by the earth. They worshipped the Great Spirit no less than did the Christian, the Hindu, or the Muslim; and felt Him in everything around them. Today, by contrast, these blessings of our environment are treated as a source of profit, and are so abused that they have to be guarded by militant preservation and protection societies and 'green' groups trying to stop the plunder and despoliation of nature. Their zeal may sometimes cause damage. But underlying it is a vague feeling that these things belong to the Nation (etymo-logically 'born of the same stock': cf. 'clan' below). But few, if any, seem to appreciate that this is precisely where, by Natural and by Divine Law, the property in them lies.

Aboriginal peoples, so near to nature, had a deep affinity with their natural surroundings. They realized they were land creatures. They had to have land to live on, and land to live from. They worshipped the spirits of wood and stream, hill and dale, and had no conception of a landowner charging his fellow human beings for access to them. This gave them an intuitive feeling for Natural Law, which is observable in the clash between the white man and the men of other colours in Africa, America, and New Zealand, in whose territories they settled.

Title to land is obtained either by discovery of virgin land, or (as Scripture reminds us) by conquest of prior settlers. Both can usefully be called 'colonization'. In this sense England was colonized sporadically by Celts, Romans, Saxons, Danes, and Vikings in succession. Subsequently William the Conqueror took over the country as a whole, and present title to English land stems from his conquest; most of the land, of course, being left in possession of its former Saxon occupants, under Norman overlords. This pattern is surprisingly similar to the history of aboriginal peoples.

The Coming of the Maori[16] describes three waves of settlement of New Zealand. The first arrivals found no-one to oppose their settlement. During the second settlement there were some changes of ownership through conquest, but there was more than enough land to allow the developing tribes to find new areas for peaceful occupation. The third settlers established themselves on different parts of the coast, built their houses and villages, and cleared the land for their cultivation. They came into conflict with the earlier inhabitants and extended their territory by conquest and occupation. This description almost tallies with that of The English Settlements by the Angles, Saxons, Jutes and Frisians. It is indeed the process of colonization all over the world. But the subsequent history, in the nations which have become highly developed through trade, industry, commerce, and finance is different indeed from that of the aboriginal peoples.

> [The Maori] system of community co-operation in cultivation and sharing the natural resources of their territory inhibited any trend towards individualism and the individual ownership of land. The land belonged to the sub-tribe and the tribe ... The individual had his share of the common ownership, but he could not be said to own any particular portion of it in perpetuity. He had the use of particular portions and his neighbours respected his allotment as he respected theirs. He had the use of it during his lifetime, and his heirs had the use of it during their lifetime ... Maori lands occupied the same position as entailed estates and could not be alienated by individuals. Thus they formed a fluid asset which could be adjusted to meet the varying needs of succeeding generations ...
> The early chiefs bemused by the rattle of hoop iron and tin pannikins, sold large areas of tribal land for the cheap products of English factories. It has been said that the chiefs and people thought they were merely giving the newcomers the right to use the land, not realizing that they were parting with their tribal heritage for ever. Probably this is true of the early sales.[17]

The story of the meeting of the white and the black cultures in Africa is not so clear as to the origins of the tribes, but the same "fundamental difference in the European and African attitudes to land-tenure is apparent. Amongst the African Negro communities land is held to be inalienable and incapable of transfer by purchase ... Unfortunately this difference was not appreciated by white settlers or by colonial governments until after some of the best land had passed out of native title and occupation. This more than anything else probably accounts for the detribalization of native society throughout Africa south of the Sahara".[18]

African land-tenure laws seem to fall into a general pattern of which the Lozi tribe who dwell in the great flood plain of the Upper Zambezi River are strikingly representative. ... Ultimately the Lozi consider that all the land, and its products, belong to the nation through the King. Though one right of Lozi citizenship, to which all men who are accepted as subjects are entitled, is a right to building and to arable land and a right to use public lands for grazing and fishing, it is by the King's bounty that his subjects live on and by the land. Commoners think of themselves as permanently indebted to the King for the land on which they live and its wild and domesticated products which sustain them. The Lozi say this is why they gave tribute and service to him and still give gifts ...[19]

(p 38) To balance his rights and powers, the King is under a duty to do certain things with the land. He is obliged to give every subject land to live on and land to cultivate ... Should he [himself] desire land he must ask for it: 'The King is also a beggar'." - [Cf. Eccl. 5: 9. 'Moreover the profit of the earth is for all: the King himself is served by the field']

(p 40) The King may be called 'owner of the land' only as trustee or steward for the nation. He granted a primary estate of rights of administration to all titles of heads of villages, including himself in his capacity as head of many villages. Each head of a village then broke his estate into secondary estates with rights of administration which he allotted to heads of households in the village including himself. These holders of secondary estates might allocate tertiary estates of this kind to dependent heads of household, but usually broken up and allocated in parcels of land to be worked as arable, or as fishing sites by the holders ... Landholding in these tribes is thus an inherent attribute not only of citizenship, but also of each social position in the political and kinship hierarchy.

The American Red Indians had the same kind of attitude to land:

In America, the land within the tribal boundaries was regarded as belonging to the tribe. Neither the Indian individual nor the family possessed vested rights in land, although each family might appropriate or have assigned to it, for cultivation or gathering, that required for its own needs. Thus it was impossible for any chief, family, or any section of a tribe legally to sell or give away any part of the tribal holdings. Naturally any such treaties and transfers of rights had no significance to the early Indians. The first white settlers either were not aware of this fact or found it convenient to ignore it.[20]

The difference between the two cultures arises from the modern assumption that society is a collection of individuals. Tribal society by contrast was a collection of families. An aggregation of families formed an extended family (or *gens* to use the Roman word). The aggregation of *gentes* formed the Tribe. The aggregation of Tribes constituted the Commonwealth. The consanguinity was real in the family, but in the extension to *gens* and tribe, included a number of incomers who, by a legal fiction, feigned themselves to be descended from the same stock as the people on whom they were grafted.[21]

The feeling for land, and their relationship to it as a family, can be illustrated closer to home and to our own time. Members of the Gaelic clan (clann or clanna, meaning children) were regarded as descended from a common ancestor, actual or mythical. The Chief was parent, ruler, and landowner on behalf of the clan. Chief is a territorial title. It was the duty of the chief to ensure all the clan were possessed of land enough to live on and from. The succession to the chiefship was hereditary, the successor being appointed from among nine of the dying chief's nearest kinsmen. There were also chieftains each representing a branch of the clan.[22] This close cohesion and provision of a livelihood for all is a long way from present-day social organisation and practice.

There is a remarkable similarity in English Land law. In Alfred's time folc land was land held on customary tenure, and boc land was land allotted on terms contained in a charter or 'book'. The first tended to be held by the common people, the second by thegns and other nobility. But the essence of both was that the land was held in return for services or payment which had to be made to the King. After the conquest the land was held of a Lord, who himself held, sometimes through other Lords, but in any case ultimately of the King, and always in return for rent in the form of services or money - "no land without a Lord". The modern law *in theory* forbids any private person from owning more than a freehold tenancy from the Crown. This is in great contrast to absolute ownership (*dominium*) under continental European systems.

In practice, however, land is bought and sold exactly as if the possessor had *dominium*. This fundamental change came about gradually as the law over the years released all the common law inhibitions on alienation of land out of the family. The result was a disaster to the Exchequer. The loss of the land-rents forced the Crown into peacetime taxation as we shall see in Part II, and when that proved insufficient, into more and more borrowing. The cost in interest exacerbated the situation into a vicious circle. Moreover the state had ultimately to take over the care of the large number of families who were made landless, and so deprived of a place to live and a place from which to draw on the earth's resources for a living.

Anglo-Saxon England

England before the Conquest presents a very different picture. The Germanic tribes who succeeded the Romans in occupying Britain had one thing in common. They were regarded by the Romans as outer barbarians. They had not been affected by contact with Rome, as had the Franks who had fought both for and against the Roman Emperors. This accounts for a good deal of the difference between France and England today. Angles, Saxons, Jutes, and Frisians were imbued with the traditional freedom of primitive German society. They were loyal to their leader, but recognised no authority between the leader and themselves. Once settled in Britain their leader was king. In the 6th to 8th centuries the large number of such kings had gradually reduced to the Heptarchy: Mercia, Anglia, Kent, Wessex and so on. The *ceorl*, or free peasant, formed the basis of society. He was the independent master of a peasant household, whose position was protected by the King's law. He had no claim to nobility, but was subject to no lord below the king.[23]

In the laws of Ine (689-726), which is our earliest document that throws light on agricultural practice, there is no mention of any lord having control of country life below the king. The ceorl was a free man amongst freemen with whom he co-operated in farming the land, and sharing the available woods, springs, marshes, rough ground and other feedings as well as fisheries. Any disputes between them were subject to adjudication only by or on behalf of the king. It is almost certain that by law and custom the 'family land' could not be alienated so as to bypass expectant heirs. Slavery was part of the early English law, and the ceorl was usually a slave owner. But his slaves were probably not of his own race, and certainly not of his own tribe.

There is no trace of nobility amongst these invading tribes, except the nobility of the kingly family. But round the king were gathered his *gesiths* - companions: the bond between lord and man - the duty of defending and avenging a lord, the disgrace of surviving him - was a well-known feature of Germanic tradition, and this they brought to Britain. There was a line of demarcation between the *gesiths* and the ceorls evidenced by their worth in terms of the wergild to be paid in a case of manslaughter. In the laws of Ine the *gesithcund* man's wergild was 1,200 shillings, as against the 200 shilling wergild of the ceorl.

This was an age of freedom such as is beyond the comprehension of our own time. Again, how did it come about? Some light can be thrown upon the remarkable loss of freedom by examining the slow introduction in Anglo-Saxon England of customs which were precipitated by the Norman Conquest into a virtual replica of the continental feudal system.

Those gathered round the king in Saxon times had to be supported, and this was achieved by grants of newly conquered or unoccupied land. But by the late 7th century, grants were being made to the king's companions, not of land, but of the rents and services properly due to the king. At first it mattered not to the ceorl whether he paid his dues to a thegn or to the king. But as this custom grew, there were soon men of the higher class who were lords over large numbers of small villages. After such a grant the duty to repair bridges easily passed into a duty to repair the buildings of the new lord's farmstead. The king's dues were brought to him there. This was the origin of the Manor which features so persistently in Domesday.

Subsequently, the idea grew that the landlord needed written evidence of his rights, and this by Alfred's time (871-899) had become familiar as 'book'- (viz. charter-) land. Boc-land could be granted exempt from the common law dues in support of the king, save the *trimoda necessitas*, by which the land nearly always remained bound. It stands distinguished from folc-land, which means either common land (*ager publicus*), or more probably ordinary land, that is to say land held under ordinary custom or common law.

Ine's laws also contain passages which suggest that something like leases of land were being made between a lord and a tenant of a 'yard', viz, a quarter of a hide, of land. This was the measure of land held in medieval times by the *gebur*. Thus the Normans after the conquest found a system of land tenure by different classes which in part at least resembled the feudal system which covered continental Europe. A pre-conquest description of an estate (the *rectitudines singularum personarum*) describes the classes which had by then evolved, namely: Thegn, Genear, Cottar, and Gebur. Of these the gebur is the only one the freedom of whose position is in doubt. He was a "peasant trembling on the edge of serfdom" ... "there were innumerable men of free descent, cultivating on unalterable terms family lands which they or their ancestors had been compelled to surrender into the hands of a lord in return for relief from present necessities and in the hope of future security".[24] It seems therefore that the initial freedom of the whole tribe had already been compromised before the Conquest.

Of course those who received grants of the dues which ought to have been rendered to the king, were given them in return for service. They were very much part of the kingdom's fighting force, or its administration; of the judicial system, or of the royal household. The trouble begins, many centuries later, when through centralisation of government functions, and the employment of professionals, these underlords were relieved of their duties, but left in receipt of the dues, for which many of them did nothing in return.

One of the very clear trends which emerges from this

backward look is that the direction of the flow of money has to a very large extent over some eight or nine centuries been reversed. Six centuries ago in peacetime it was to the exchequer that money still flowed naturally. War taxes were for ever being raised, and their deficiency made up for by borrowing. It was war that emptied the public purse. But apart from customary levies on goods imported by foreign merchants (later called the customs) peacetime taxation hardly existed. The King (who was the government) was expected to "live of his own": and this meant that he had to pay the cost of central government in peacetime out of the revenue flowing naturally into his exchequer as feudal overlord. This can only be seen by taking a long view of the history of the Crown's revenues. An even longer view reveals in Saxon times a greater freedom from the oppression of central government, greater independence and self reliance, greater cohesion of local society, and dependence on central government confined principally to defence. Common Law was the crystallization of Custom; and laws promulgated by the King advised by the Witan ('wise men' - viz. his Council) were mostly only declaratory of the Common Law. Today by contrast, the exchequer in peacetime pays out more than it gets in, and the deficit has to be made up by borrowing. After over fifty years without a major war, government debt has reached an alarming level, and may yet have to increase. There are numerous families totally reliant on government support in all aspects of their lives; and with the outlook that 'they' - the 'social' or the 'council' - will put right anything that goes wrong. The natural independence and self-reliance of British peoples has been undermined.

All this has substantive implications for social policies today, upon which it would be as well to reflect before proceeding to the detailed consideration of how the "freeborn" Englishman came to be rootless in his own land. The way in which the loss of natural rights to land penetrates deep into the fabric of society must be borne in mind, for otherwise the "remedies" for social problems may be adopted that are not appropriate. To illustrate the point, in Ch. 3 we will analyse the historical background to crime and punishment, which is a controversial issue of our time. There are lessons to be learned from the Saxon system of criminal law, and the more modern system that replaced it. Looking back to early times does not solve the problem, but it identifies the origins of the problem, and this assists in formulating appropriate solutions by throwing up new ideas and new ways of looking at it. Imprisonment, in particular has been condemned for its cost, and its soul-destroying effect on nominally 'free' men and women. Capital punishment also is a recurring subject of debates, which result in nothing. But there has been little examination of history to discover how imprisonment and the death penalty came to be used in the first place as a regular punishment in criminal courts for serious crime; or how these punishments were extended far beyond what public opinion could stomach. A review of that history illuminates the underlying problem which makes itself felt in so many other spheres of our lives. That problem, in short, is the increasing erosion of our social and individual liberties as a result of losing the traditional rights of equal access to land.

3

Criminal Law since Saxon Times

The Common Law owes a great deal to its Saxon origins. One of the great virtues of the Saxon state was the judicial system of local courts. These continued long after the conquest until from the twelfth century onwards the reorganised royal courts took over more and more of the judicial work. Saxon legal remedies were by no means perfect. Some punishments we would now regard as barbarous, and things got worse after the Conquest with the introduction of the cruel Norman Forest Laws and Trial by Battle. But the concept underlying punishment in Saxon England is remarkable, and might well teach a lesson for today. The idea seems to have been: 'If you don't keep the rules of the club, then you lose the right to its benefits; and if the matter is serious enough you must be asked to leave, or expelled'. It is interesting that this same philosophy in modern times has inspired the trade unions' rule books in their treatment of discipline - fines, loss of benefit, and expulsion. In Old English law except for High and Petty treason, the usual punishments for serious crime were banishment, outlawry, abjuration of the realm, or monetary penalties, even for manslaughter and murder[25]. "Imprisonment would have been regarded in these old times as a useless punishment;

it does not satisfy revenge, it keeps the criminal idle, and, do what we may it is costly. Imprisonment was not thought of as a common law punishment".[26]

After Henry II established the circuit system, his judges used imprisonment as a means of ensuring the presence of the defendant at the trial, and to compel obedience to orders of the court. The judges on circuit all over the country assumed power to imprison indefinitely after conviction. It swiftly became their practice to use this power to extract money from the defendant:

> The justices do not want to keep him in gaol, they wish to make him pay money. [After 1215 they had no power to fine. The imposition of a fine would have been an evasion of Magna Carta. But] What the judges can do is this:- they can pronounce a sentence of imprisonment and then allow the culprit to 'make fine', that is to say make an end (*finem facere*) of the matter by paying or finding security for a certain sum of money. In theory the fine is a bilateral transaction, a bargain; it is not 'imposed' it is 'made' ... The wrongdoer rarely goes to prison even for a moment. On the plea roll the *custodiatur* which sends him to gaol is followed at once by *Finem fecit per unam marcam* (or whatever the sum may be), and then come the names of the those who are pledges for the payment.[27]

We point out later that the mediaeval courts, far from costing money, were at one time a source of considerable revenue to the Crown. In Plantagenet times when the Kings took over the local jurisdictions, receipts from 'fines and amercements' in the King's courts brought in revenue which was dubbed a *magnum emolumentum* of the Crown. By Elizabeth's reign, the introduction of imprisonment had reduced this to about £2000, although even that was not a small sum in those days. It certainly makes one wonder how such a lucrative system could have turned into today's administration of justice which is a considerable drain on the exchequer to be met by the taxpayer, with legal aid alone costing (1996) £1.4 billion a year. Surely a consideration of legal history would bring a little more light to the debates on this subject. The flow of money should be towards the Crown, not towards the criminal. How did this come about?

In Saxon times, and later, death was a rare sentence, even for murder. It was usually redeemable by a suitable money payment. In Northumberland in 1256, out of seventy seven convicted murderers, only four were hanged, although in that rather wild county most of the others were outlawed. Imprisonment was a means of keeping the prisoner secure whilst awaiting trial. Serious crime was visited with banishment, with lands escheating to the Crown. Failure to appear in court brought outlawry - the loss of the law's protection. Fines and forfeitures were a commonplace punishment. The flow of money was from the wrongdoers to the Crown. Statutes of Edward I freely distributed short terms of imprisonment in local gaols. But even in these cases the longest imprisonment was three years, and was as a general rule preparatory to a fine, i.e. a money payment to make an end (*finem*) of it. The Statute of Westminster I (1275: chapters 9, 13, 15, 29, 31, and 32) deal with the duty to pursue felons, the ravishing of women, unlawful bailment, excessive tolls (40 days imprisonment), and purveyors to the Crown not paying for what they take.

Chapter 20 is interesting. It was made necessary because the baron who had formerly "lived with his warriors on a mound behind a ditch lay far behind. Now he was a country gentleman, passed from one house to another, and enjoyed the amenity of parks and fishponds."[28] Chapter 20 ordered trespassers upon enclosed private fishponds and parks to be imprisoned for three years, and then if they could not pay their fines, to abjure the realm.

Today the burden of private debt makes the old punishments impracticable. As already indicated building societies and banks as mortgagees own most of the private housing, and finance companies own many of the expensive chattels provided under hire-purchase or similar arrangements. The result is that the courts cannot forfeit the motor bikes, television sets, music centres etc. of young offenders, or the houses and furniture of the more prosperous. Instead, over the last half century, expensive provision has been made to avoid imprisoning young people. They have been confined in Borstals, Reform Schools, Detention Centres (mild or tough); or put into care in hostels, or under local authority social workers, or probation officers. The cost is high. The taxpayer pays. Victims of crime have to be compensated too. Again the taxpayer pays through the Criminal Injuries Compensation Board. Would not a new light be shed, and a new direction given to the argument if more attention were directed to the ancient powers of the Sheriffs to seize and sell the criminal's chattels on behalf of the Crown? How would public opinion react to this? Or to the idea of criminals, as a kind of partial outlawry, losing part of their entitlement to welfare benefit - income support for example - on conviction for multiple burglaries? The trend has swung between deterrence and reform; between education and punishment. But little notice has been taken of history as a guide to what could be done.

Substantial fines are mostly used for punishing motorists; and this causes resentment when they are treated more harshly than burglars. When real criminal offences are dealt with by fine, most Magistrates' Courts today have to set aside one day's sitting each week for fine enforcement. They have to deal with defendants who have a number of small unpaid fines outstanding. They often find it impossible to recover any substantial amount of the money due. That has to be set against the cost of sittings and their administration. At the trial there would often have been witnesses giving enthusiastic evidence in favour of the defendant and his good character. They are not called upon to write a cheque to keep their protégé out of prison. Their forefathers would have had to pledge the money to obtain his freedom.

Apart from short prison sentences expected, as already mentioned, to be brought to an end by payment of a fine,

> Imprisonment as a punishment has had a place in the British penal system for a comparatively short time, although prisons have been used throughout history by those who would be rid of their enemies or confine an embarrassing rival. Every mediaeval castle had its dungeons for the incarceration of enemies or the punishment of idle serfs. But this was a private or political use of imprisonment ... The first use of prison as a means of punishment came at the end of the 16th century when the vagrancy laws provided

for the imprisonment of those who were idle or found wandering.[29]

Why then were there people at this time in England idle and wandering? Had they no work to do? Had they no homes to go to? "Hark, hark, the dogs bark, the beggars are coming to town!" They had been turned out of their villages, out of their homes, and from the land they worked, by the enclosures. These had been going on sporadically for a long time, but had been accelerated by the Black Death of 1346/7, and the Wars of the Roses following the Hundred Years War. The vagrancy laws arose out of "the great question which agitated rural England in the sixteenth century - the question of the enclosures".[30] The early Tudors attempted to deal with them by prohibitive Statutes, but without success. Wolsey appointed 15 commissions to enquire into them, but with no result. By Elizabeth's reign the problem had become explosive.[31]

> The great floating population of vagabonds who used [the roads] presented a problem which could not be ignored. Here the need for action on a nationwide scale was more than ever apparent, for in spite of all previous attempts to control the plague of beggars their numbers had increased so greatly as to constitute a grave menace to public order ... the 'vagabonds' or 'sturdy beggars' alone numbered 10,000 ... There were no fewer than twenty-three categories of thieves and swindlers ... Such was the composition of this 'merry England' that slept in hay lofts, sheepcotes, or on doorsteps, spreading terror in the country and disease in the towns.

The official attitude to the whole fraternity of vagabonds had always been, and still was, one of fear-ridden ferocity: they were the true 'caterpillars of the commonwealth', who lick the sweat from the labourers' brows. But the impotent poor, the poor by casualty, who were 'poor in very deed', were acknowledged to be a charge on public benevolence.

Pauper enactments in 1563 and 1572 eventually established the rating system to support the 'impotent, aged and needy'. "For the rogues it was whipping, and in the last resort if they continued in their roguery, death for felony".[32] The descendants of the dispossessed, wrenched from their connection with the land, and often parted from their families, were sucked into the towns to work, if they could get work, and to inhabit slums. Within a few generations respectable families were reduced to working as wage slaves, or having to live by their wits.

From this time forward capital punishment became more and more common. As a result of rigorous Tudor and Stuart enactments to curb the menace of rogues and vagabonds rendered landless by ecclesiastical and lay enclosures, in Charles II's reign (1668) about 50 offences carried the death penalty, and transportation began. By the eighteenth century "almost all serious crimes (felonies) were punishable with death, but only a small proportion of those who were convicted of felony were actually executed. The majority of those sentenced to death were pardoned by the King, but their pardon was granted on condition that they consent to be transported to one of the colonies where labour was required - in the 17th and 18th centuries this was America, and following American independence, Australia. Eventually the courts were given power to pronounce sentences of transportation themselves".[33]

Transportation represents a terrible extension of the Saxon ideas of 'outlawry' and 'abjuring the realm'. The procedure at its inception harks back to the 'bargain' made by the judges in earlier centuries to allow the prisoner to pay for his release from prison. The horrors of imprisonment in the hulks anchored in the river Thames are well enough known. Transportation became impossible when the American War of Independence broke out, but the sentences of transportation continued to be passed until, according to Burke, 100,000 untransported prisoners were being retained in gaol, with 558 of them packed into Newgate. Not until 1784 did Parliament authorise the prescription by Order in Council of 'any place it thought fit as a penal colony'. The Botany Bay expedition arrived in Australia in 1787.

Again, when capital punishment is debated today, although 19th century history is often referred to, little attention is given to how and why the death sentence became so frequent. In 1821 Sir Thomas Buxton told the House of Commons:

> Men there are living today, at whose birth our code contained less than 70 capital offences; and we have seen that number trebled. It is a fact that there stand upon our code 150 offences, made capital during the last century. It is a fact that 600 men were condemned to death last year upon statutes passed within that century. And it is a fact that a great proportion of those who were executed were executed on statutes thus comparatively recent.

This was at a time when parliament had completely changed its policy. Enclosure Acts under the Tudors were Acts to *prevent* enclosure. Now they had become Acts to *authorize* enclosures, which were turning more and more of the common people out of their villages to make way for 'improvement'. The General Report of the Board of Agriculture on Enclosures[34] gives the acreage enclosed from the time of Queen Anne down to 1805 as 4,187,056.

Closer to Nature, Closer to God

The sickness of society today is the result of a falling away from Nature. Man no longer has an affinity with the land and his environment. He is divorced from them. The very word 'land' has come to be used for the broad country acres, there for all to see, whilst the land which has disappeared under buildings as towns and cities grew ever larger passed into oblivion. Yet it was town land that yielded the greater wealth, and city land the greatest to those who work on it. Working in Lombard Street produces far, far more wealth (no matter who gets it) than working on a Welsh hillside. The strictly *country* landowner today is often a relatively poor man.

People feel the loss, and long to be closer to Nature. Wrenched from what he knows as 'land', the first desire in the heart of a successful townsman is to find a place in the country where he can pretend to be a countryman. The poorer office and factory workers, who haven't the means to do that, flee to 'get away from it all' for holidays at home or abroad in places where society is more primitive. As Marcus Aurelius wrote in his *Meditations*:

Men seek out retreats for themselves, cottages in the country, lonely seashores and mountains. Thou too art disposed to hanker after such things: and yet all this is the commonest stupidity; for it is in thy power, whenever thou wilt, to retire into thyself: and nowhere is there any place whereunto a man may retire quieter and more free from politics than his own soul; above all if he have within him thoughts such as he may regard attentively to be at perfect ease: and that ease is nothing else than a well-ordered mind.[35]

This indicates the way back to individual sanity, and to a healthy society. History shows how Greed, Envy, Wrath, Pride and Lust have powered wars, rebellions, and the snatching and seizing of land among all classes. What is needed is a change of mind - a *metanoia*, especially among our rulers. But since our rule is ultimately to a certain extent democratic, the change has to be in at least a considerable body of people. We need a society without deceit: where people think as they feel, speak as they think, and do as they say. But from the very start the feeling has to be pure. The devices and desires of our hearts have to be watched, and we need a defence from our enemies - the desires which are inimical to us. It is the Church which should be giving the lead in this. They have the custody of the scriptures and the duty of explaining them. They used regularly to teach the divine law including Thou shalt not steal; which means we should take from the universe only what we deserve, considering everyone else as equally deserving. If we take and accumulate extra, that is theft - theft from the divinely created universe. We should not take anything more than is available to everybody else.

Helped by the Church to right feeling, right thinking should follow, with the intellectual classes genuinely exploring the means of bringing the scriptural teaching into practice.

Those who speak - in today's world the media are the mouth of the body politic - should carry right thinking into right speaking; and those who rule us could then carry this into right action in legislation and administration.

It has to be through a well-ordered mind which accepts the teaching of religion that the motherland is our common inheritance, allotted to all; through philosophy, bidding us share the gifts of Nature, and the blessings of co-operation which comes to us from the rest of the community. Since these gifts and blessings fall in different degree on each inhabited spot; science has to search diligently for the Justice of what is nowadays called a 'level playing field'. This is a condition where the opportunity anyone has is equal to that of everyone else, because he shares equally with everyone else in the common inheritance. What good he makes of it, how hard or efficiently he works is his concern alone. In such a society, where the natural rights of the individual have been restored to create a meaningful system of liberty, 'Welfare' is only necessary to support those who are so severely disabled in body or mind that they cannot be expected to work. The fiscal basis of such a society will be considered in more detail after first investigating in depth the process by which our communities were impoverished and our primary civil liberty (that of access to nature) was eliminated.

PART II

English Land Law
& Public Revenue

4

The Descent into Chaos

The law governing the use and disposition of land in England today bears indelible traces of its rich history spanning more than ten centuries. These traces are the relics of a system of landholding which provided for government, and the revenue to support it, at every level from villager to King. During those centuries, decrees of Kings, statutes of parliament, decisions of judges, and the work of administrators, acting under political, social, and economic pressures, have gradually and inexorably changed landholding into a system for personal enrichment of those able to take advantage of the unique value of property in land. It is proposed here to state the law as it is today, to show how it came to be as it is, and to consider what we may learn from its history, in dealing with contemporary problems.

Professor Sir William Holdsworth, the pre-eminent historian of the law, pointed out in relation to land:

> The rules which regulate the manner in which land can be owned, and used, and disposed of, must always be of the very greatest importance to the state. The stability of the state and the wellbeing of its citizens at all times depend,

to no small extent, on its land law. This is as true today as it was in the earlier period of our history.[1]

The earliest cultures were in no doubt as to the truth of this - the food gatherers, the keepers of sheep, the hunters, and the tillers of the soil. In passing through these stages of development, Man never lost sight of his utter dependence on land and the resources of nature to which land gave access. One of the chief features of the unfolding story of land is war; and it is worth remembering that war began when, of the sons of Adam, "Abel was a keeper of sheep, but Cain was a tiller of the ground". Cain, one may suppose, having laboured to improve the land, would have been zealous to protect what he considered to be 'his'. Otherwise he could not reap what he had sown. Agriculture made it imperative to hold land, so as not to lose the fruits of his labour.

All aboriginal peoples felt their closeness to the land, often looking upon it as their Mother. The highly civilized ancient Athenians boasted that they were *autochthonous* (sprung from the soil), and Socrates made use of the legend of Cadmus in Plato's *Republic*.[2] In Plato's *Laws* (740) land was to be distributed so that each man receiving his portion should regard it as the common property of the whole City, and tend it more carefully than children would tend their mother.

It was only as mankind advanced beyond a subsistence economy, first to trading in market towns, then to commerce in provincial centres, and so on to national and then international financing in cities, that the most valuable land disappeared beneath buildings to be lost sight of except by land speculators, who reaped a richer harvest from it in money than any agriculturist ever did in crops. Unfortunately, when people spoke of land they usually meant country land, and overlooked the vital importance of land in towns and cities. This was particularly unfortunate because the land on which buildings stood was, and has always remained, by far the most valuable. It is measured in square feet rather than in broad acres.

Our Anglo-Saxon ancestors when they first occupied England more than a thousand years ago paid little attention to the highly civilized towns left behind by the Romans. Later on they found them useful as forts against the incursions of subsequent invaders, especially the Danes. They also established *byrig* (forts) of their own which, in later times when they were not under threat, developed into trading posts, as did the landing places which they fortified. The latter became 'ports', and the Saxon *bihr* grew into the medieval 'borough' - while the wealth of both increased mightily.

In the overwhelmingly agricultural society of the Saxons the status of every individual was determined by his landholding; and custom, backed up where necessary by law, imposed upon him the duty to render (Lat. *reddere*, give back) service or wealth in return for the land he held. Thus public revenue normally came from the productivity of land, in the form of food-rent, rent service, or rent in money or kind. Taxation was theoretically, and perhaps in practice, only raised to meet emergencies, although invasions, particularly by Danes, made taxation a pretty regular event. It too was assessed on land, not simply by area, but with due regard to fertility and situation so as to ensure that good land rendered more in tax than poor land. Our fiscal history over the millennium since then will show that:

(1) The productivity of land gradually ceased to be the measure of the contribution due from the individual to cover the expenses of government.

(2) The consequent impoverishment of the Crown drove kings and parliaments to raise money by arbitrary taxation levied upon anything other than land that would 'bear the tax'; and this they did in times of peace as well as of war.

(3) Finding it impossible to raise sufficient revenue by these means, especially to pay for war, the Crown very soon had to resort to borrowing to make up the deficiency.

(4) The Jews, who commanded the realm of finance and especially international finance, lent money to the Crown at very high rates of interest. After their expulsion in 1290, English merchants, who were becoming increasingly wealthy, continued the practice.

(5) This was because those who retained land, free of any duty to contribute to the public purse, were now in a position to lend their surplus wealth to the state in return for interest. They lent what they had hitherto been duty-bound to render to the King - the interest they received always adding further to public expenditure, and so increasing taxation.

(6) The taxation not being assessed on land was paid by rich and poor alike, the burden falling more heavily on the poor, some of whom, particularly in times of

plague or dearth, were driven from the little land they held. 'Rogues' and 'Vagabonds' became statutory expressions to describe them in Vagrancy Acts after 1572.

(7) Inevitably charitable opinion began to insist that the landless poor should be supported out of public funds, and this in the sixteenth century gave rise to the Poor Law, given final statutory expression in 1601. The burden of poor relief increased when the parliamentary enclosures of the eighteenth and early nineteenth centuries swelled the number of landless, and that burden has continued to increase until the present time under the euphemistic titles 'Welfare' and 'Social Security'.

Political power right up until the nineteenth century rested quite naturally with the landed: not only with the kings who were great landowners, but also with their head tenants, the 'barons', until the Wars of the Roses weakened the barons both politically and financially. After the civil war in the 17th century Parliament became the supreme fount of law, and two classes fought to control it: the 'squirearchy', whose power was based largely on country land; and the 'mercantile class', whose wealth came from the towns, where some had a freehold, but many were leaseholders. Representation in parliament was based on a property qualification. Fear of revolution such as had occurred in France at the end of the 18th century was averted in the 19th century by the Reform Acts. The first of these Acts retained a property qualification for voting, but later Acts gave the landless voting power for the first time without their having any interest in land. They had power without responsibility. Inevitably in the twentieth century that power has been used to widen immensely the scope of poor relief and other public expenditure to such an extent that in our own day the burden of its cost is becoming almost impossible to bear, and the moral deterioration of those who cannot (and some who will not) support themselves is now becoming apparent. The conclusion of this process was neatly summed up by Goldsmith in *The Deserted Village*:

> Ill fares the land to hastening ills a prey.
> Where wealth accumulates and men decay.

5

Origin & Growth of the Land Law

The law relating to land as it stands today is set out in a standard textbook as follows:

> The basis of English land law is that all land in England is owned by the Crown. A small part is in the Crown's actual occupation; the rest is occupied by tenants holding, either directly or indirectly from the Crown. *"Nulle terre sans seigneur"* (no land without a lord): there is no *allodial* land in England, i.e. no land owned by a subject and not held of some lord.[3]

Allodium is a Frankish word meaning 'entire property' (O.E.D.). It is distinguished from a feu or fee, also Frankish, which lay at the heart of the feudal system, and it is from the feudal system and the Norman Conquest that our present-day land law derives. Although the feudal system existed in Anglo-Saxon England, the extent of it at that time is still a matter of controversy. The important point is that the 'entire property' in land - allodium - was simply not available to any individual either in Saxon times or after the Conquest, and this position remains the same today. Saxon kings would not grant land without the approval of the Witan. William I, by contrast, regarded the whole of England as his by conquest, and accordingly granted lands to his followers as a reward for their services; but only upon certain conditions, which constituted rent, usually in kind or in service, but sometimes (and increasingly so) in money.

Those who held directly of the King were called tenants *in capite* (in chief). The land they themselves occupied was their demesne land: the rest they granted away on mesne tenure to tenants who held indirectly from the Crown on similar conditions, and the mesne tenants might in turn have tenants under them, in a line of sub-infeudation, but all rendering to their immediate lord rent-service or rent in money or in kind for the land they held. These tenants-in-chief and some of their mesne tenants who held by military tenure, were called 'barons', a word meaning simply 'the boys' or 'men' - the Conqueror's men, the Earl's men, and so on. Later, the word was confined to the King's men, viz. the tenants-in-chief. 'Baron' was not a title, and gave no indication of rank, although it did denote a powerful position as tenant in capite. The first barony created by patent as a rank was in 1387; the next (in 1431) was the beginning of regular creations of this kind. Even today the title purports to designate a connection with land: for example 'Baron Jenkins of Ashley Gardens'.

The one abiding addition to the tenures of Saxon land law made by the Conqueror was military tenure by knight service. The head tenant had to provide a certain number (usually in multiples of five) of armed horsemen to serve in the royal army for 40 days in the year. He might in turn exact knight service from or parcel out some of his own quota of service to his mesne tenants. This was the result of the partitioning of England among a foreign (Norman) aristocracy organized for war. It only concerned the upper layers of landed gentry, who, as head tenants or mesne tenants, had to provide the service of so many knights for so many days when called upon to do so. Beneath this superimposed duty of military service, the old Saxon land law remained.

The same standard textbook (p. 24) puts the law at the present day succinctly:

> There are thus two basic doctrines in the law of real property. These are known as:-
>
> (1) the doctrine of tenures: all land is held of the crown, either directly or indirectly, on one or other of the various tenures; and
>
> (2) the doctrine of estates: a subject cannot own land, but can merely own an estate in it, authorizing him to hold it for some period of time.

The 'various' tenures mentioned above were not finally established until after the Norman conquest. William I began his reign in the hope of associating Frenchmen and Englishmen in his government on equal terms. But it was not to be. Forfeitures of the estates of those who fought against him at Hastings, lapse of the titles of those who died in that battle, further forfeitures after the revolt prompting the Harrowing of the North in 1069 - 70, and a further revolt in 1075, meant that: "by the end of the Conqueror's reign all directive power within the English state had passed from native into alien hands. In 1087, with less than half a dozen exceptions, every lay lord whose possessions entitled him to political influence was a foreigner".[4]

Thus under the feudal system in England the most a man could have was an estate in land of which he had tenure (Lat. *tenere* - to hold) from a lord, to whom he rendered services or paid money, and who in his turn rendered similarly to his lord and so on up through a line of sub-infeudation headed by the Crown as supreme overlord.

The free services were four: spiritual (frankalmoin), military (knight service), personal (serjeanty), and miscellaneous (socage). These came under the protection of the common law. The unfree services were in villeinage (later called copyhold), consisting largely of labour. Unfree service was theoretically at the will of the lord of the unfree tenant, although in practice defined and protected by the custom of the manor as administered in the manor court. In the fourteenth century it began to be called 'copyhold' because the conditions of tenure were evidenced by a 'copy' of the manor court roll. In the fifteenth, the king's courts began to protect copyholders, and copyholders were more and more commuting their rent services into money.

Free tenure was also subject to *Incidents*, listed by Blackstone as aids, relief, primer seisin, wardship, marriage, fines for alienation, and escheat. These need not be further described, but it is very important to stress that they constituted a considerable source of revenue, especially to the Crown - the supreme or head landlord - and that it was a revenue issuing out of the land. Accordingly although in the course of time the services due from the various kinds of free tenure came to be of very little value, they continued to exist so as to preserve the incidents of those tenures, which were so very valuable to the king. Tenure by Knight-service, for example, was only abolished by a statute of 1660, although by the end of the 13th century, the service was no longer called for.

The whole system was bound together in a close structure by the Domesday Survey ordered in 1085, and completed within a year from information obtained at inquests before sworn juries all over the country. It was made into a book later. Domesday was a remarkable analysis of the economic resources available to provide the Crown with revenue. Unfortunately it was not kept up to date, and inevitably as time went by the exactions by the kings, in services and in money, bore less and less relationship to the true situation of the kingdom

> Tenure [of land] carried with it reciprocal obligations and rights on the part of lord and tenant. The lord was bound to defend his tenant's title, and the tenant was bound to render to his lord certain services.[5]

This statement encapsulates the genesis of feudalism all over Europe in the early middle ages. It involved *commendatio* and *beneficium* - service in return for protection, in the face of migrant pressure from the East, and the local wars resulting from it. England, however, differed from the rest of Europe, because as an island it had sea to protect its frontiers against Europe, and because it had acquired a strong monarchy served by an efficient administration. Alone in Europe England had a state treasury and a national system of taxation (the geld). William took over both as his first action after Hastings. He continued after the conquest to levy the Saxon geld, and relied on the existing Saxon administration. This later proved strong enough, following the death of Henry II in 1189, to survive and to continue with the essentials of government whilst kings were absent from the realm (Richard), involved in civil war and foreign invasion (John), less than ten years of age on accession and embroiled again in civil war (Henry III). Indeed that unsettled period saw many striking developments in administration.

> The vitality of English institutions, resilient even during this period, is attributable to the fact that there had been established at an amazingly early date, an administration which was proof against disruptive shocks, and against swift changes in the political outlook. It is a matter of deep interest that even at this period trained men of the royal administration - the professional civil servants - remain at their posts, no matter whether kings or barons are in control.[6]

Sir William Holdsworth points to another important difference between England and the continent of Europe in the development of the feudal system. In England,

> The doctrine of tenure is a doctrine of universal application in the land law. It was applied to the free tenures, and to unfree tenure, and to the relation of lessor and lessee for years ... The fact that this doctrine of tenure was applied universally to the land law is a purely English phenomenon. Other countries knew feudal tenure; but the law governing it was applicable only to noble or military tenure.[7]

Thus as developed in England, the tenure of land was,

by its services and incidents, the main source of public revenue. From the conquest to the thirteenth century, it provided the means of fulfilling most of the functions which we now consider to be functions of central government. The feudal tenant held the land in return for rendering services which were clearly of a public nature. Providing armed knights to serve in the royal army for forty days a year is only one example. The king's butler, sword-bearer, household officials, both high and low, held land in return for the services appropriate to their various functions. In the same way provision was made for the supply of such things as military transport, weapons, and victuals for the royal court and the royal army. The Church was similarly supported in all its activities out of services rendered in return for land. In short, the whole social, economic and political structure of England in Anglo-Saxon and Norman times, and to a lessening extent for long thereafter, was based on land. The land a man held determined his position in society, his political power, and the extent of his contribution to the public revenue.

After the conquest money payments increasingly took the place of services in discharging the dues inherent in feudal land tenure. This trend ran parallel with the growth of leasing. Military tenure by knight service in particular had become obsolescent before the end of the Conqueror's reign, and payment of scutage (shield-money) in lieu of actual service began before the 11th century ended. The kings preferred it. Rufus and Henry I hired mercenaries for their foreign campaigns. Henry II professed himself 'unwilling to trouble the rustic knights'.[8] A force of knights who only had to serve forty days a year was useless in foreign campaigns, and at home a paid army was more useful in coping with baronial disorder.[9] Knights preferred to pay scutage rather than serve. Scutage thus, although a feudal due, became a kind of tax to finance wars. However it was not made into a regular tax. Its usefulness declined because the king was not strong enough to compel the barons to increase their money payment in line with inflation of the currency and the increases in the cost of soldiers and their equipment. Magna Carta put an end to John's attempts to do so. Scutage was remitted by Richard II, but because of the necessity to preserve the revenue from feudal incidents, was not abolished until 1660, by the Statute of Tenures.

Serjeanty (personal service) lasted longer. It provided all sorts of domestic service and minor government duties at court, and supplied the feudal army with light auxiliary troops, with attendance on the knights, with military material, and with transport. It decayed in the thirteenth, and especially in the fourteenth centuries, when contracts with hired servants took its place, and only a few services, mostly ceremonial, survived.

Meanwhile, the courts of common law gradually assimilated the law of copyhold (unfree tenure) to the law of free tenure. More and more land was being enclosed from the common fields into 'farms' - that is, lands held at a rent from the superior tenant. A series of nineteenth century statutes hastened the end of copyhold, and it was finally abolished by the Property Act of 1922.

The Statute of Tenures (1660) also abolished feudal incidents other than escheat and relief, and converted knight service into tenure by socage. The net result of this slow process of change in the law is that there are today only two tenures by which an estate in land can be held: one feudal - socage, now called freehold; and one traditional, namely leasehold. The Crown's feudal revenue is no longer collected. Leasehold tenants pay rent. Freehold tenants do not. This, combined with the gradual freeing of the law's restriction on the alienation of land to be mentioned later, set the scene for speculation in land which became, and is now, a legitimate means of accumulating great wealth. Although legitimate, it nevertheless contravenes the Mosaic law, and is intuitively regarded by right thinking people as wrong, even when they cannot see why. The reason is that it expropriates the revenue naturally due to the Crown.

The Crown's Revenues
The striking feature of this development of English law is that the Crown has over the years lost its revenue drawn from the land through feudal dues, feudal incidents, and gelds (a general tax on land according to its yield). We have thereby moved away from the situation where the Crown took its share of the nations wealth from individuals according to the land they possessed - the land which gave them the means with which to pay. We have now arrived at a situation where the Crown has to seek revenue by taxing anything other than land which appears to be taxable. The list over the last three centuries includes, amongst other things: tea, coffee, spices, candles, gold wire, silver wire, salt, soap, paper, calico, starch, legal deeds, newspapers, pamphlets, hearths and windows,

drink, tobacco, personal incomes, theatre and cinema tickets, and sales of the vast majority of commodities (now called VAT). None of these taxes was directed to the individual's means to pay except insofar as some of the items taxed were not in any case within the range of consumption of poorer people. Taxes on motor vehicles, which are often a necessity for poor as well as rich, have been added to the list in recent times. Taxes assessed on land have occasionally been instituted, but only for the purpose of discovering incomes, and only in conjunction with assessments of movables and personal property for the same purpose. They have never remained substantial for very long, and have lasted only to carry the burden when the assessments of movables or personal property proved impracticable. The Poor Rate of Tudor times is an exception. It lasted until it became outdated for lack of reassessment, and had to be abolished in 1990. It was, however, not truly a land tax. It was a tax on real property - buildings and land assessed together as a 'hereditament'. The Council Tax which partially replaced it is similarly based on hereditaments and is not a true land tax.

To find the origin of this remarkable switch in the source of the Crown's revenue from land to movables, thence to personal property, or to personal property and land together, in an attempt to discover peoples' incomes, we have to go back to the thirteenth century and beyond. We shall in passing also mention the occasional infliction of poll taxes as an alternative - too unpopular to be retained for long.

6

Taxation to Recoup the Crown's Lost Revenue

In Saxon times the king lived 'of his own'. He had land in his own possession. He had other sources of support either in money or in kind. He received dues from all who held land. *Feorm* (Food-rent), was due once a year from a group of villages in accordance with the general duty to maintain the King and his retinue for twenty four hours during his procession round the country. Each village was assessed at five hides, and the goods or money would be rendered at the nearest royal farm. According to Stenton there must have been a town moot of some kind to turn this arbitrary assessment into reality. There was a similar obligation to provide for the King's servants or messengers when they passed through the district on duty.

Defence was provided for by personal service in the *fyrd*. This together with the obligation to build and maintain bridges and strongholds, made up the *trimoda necessitas*. These obligations were assessed by hidage of the villages. By 1060 the renders in kind which once supported the King had been changed into money. Even by Alfred's time the royal monetary receipts were sufficient to need a central treasury under a *hraeglthegn* (chamberlain), kept from the beginning of the 11th century at Winchester.[10] There were also profits from fines and forfeitures imposed as punishment in court. We also read of church-scot, *aelmesfeoh* (alms), and hearth-penny, paid according to the status of a man in relation to his land - whether he be Thegn, Geneat, Cottar or Border, or Gebor. Slaves did not count. As already mentioned there were considerable labour services rendered within the rural economy, but always depending on landholding except in the case of slaves.

Part of the understanding that the king should 'live of his own' was that taxation should provide only for special needs, and emergencies such as war. The Danish raids and invasions of course made war a virtually constant danger, so that taxation was also fairly constant, not only for actual warfare but also for preparatory measures.

Danegeld

The most important tax was the Danegeld. *Geldan* in Anglo-Saxon means 'to yield', with which it is of course cognate. The word (three syllables, the 'g' sounding like English 'y') was, however, used to denote different kinds of levy: for example, in its literal meaning 'danegeld' was to buy off the Danes; 'heregeld' to pay for 'men' (soldiers and sailors); 'burhegeld' to fortify, maintain and man forts. It provided ships, of which a fleet of (at its biggest) forty two ships was maintained.[11]

Danegelds were levied on hides of land. Hide is 'a word of elusive meaning' (Stenton). On the authority of the Venerable Bede, a hide is defined as the amount of land needed to support a free man and his dependants (not just his family). The rate was fixed at so much a hide: in Edward the Confessor's time, it was two shillings. The hide

> varied considerably in area according to fertility, the nature of the soil, the nature of the holding, and the standard of living of the household in question. No-one would suppose, for example, that nowadays the same kind of livelihood, and therefore the same receipt to the Exchequer, would arise from 100 acres of Cheviot sheep run as from 100 acres of fenland arable.[12]

Thus Bede describes the Isle of Man (300 hides) and Anglesey (960 hides), yet their area is roughly the same. He remarks that Anglesey is more fertile. In other words a 'hide' measured not the area of land, but what it yielded. A 'geld', as its name indicates, was levied on the 'yield' of a particular parcel of land.

In general the hide denoted an area of ploughland together with its appurtenant rights in meadow, marsh, woodland, springs, fisheries, and animal grazing. Domesday Book shows 120 acres to the hide in Cambridgeshire, but only 40 in Wiltshire and Dorset. Similar variations can be found elsewhere. There was therefore some flexibility in the impact of the tax when setting a fixed rate per hide, such as two shillings. The King's financial officers (i.e. the central government) fixed the number of hides to be paid by each shire - Northants 3,000 hides, Staffs 500 hides, Worcs 1,200 hides and so on. This is to use hide in a different sense, as a unit of taxation. Here again there is flexibility. Although the number of hides per county appears to have remained fixed from pretty ancient times, there were reductions after the Battle of Hastings in the hidage of the Home Counties which had been ravaged by William in his sweep round London. Otherwise, however, the lack of regular reassessment to keep up with changing circumstances, which spoilt early tax systems, is apparent.

The Shire Courts distributed their allotted share of hides among the Hundreds, and the Hundred Courts distributed these among the villages. Although there is no evidence to show how this was done, it is reasonable to suppose that at these lower levels the courts would have taken into account current local conditions affecting ability to pay, such as flooding; disease (in men, cattle, or crops); or devastation by armies or marauders. In spite of its complication, "as a piece of large scale financial organization, it has no parallel in the dark ages. For all its apparent rigidity, it enabled the king to vary the weight and incidence of his demands as the needs of the moment required".[13] By the time of Ethelred II at latest, says Professor Stenton, we had "the first system of National Taxation in Western Europe". According to the Anglo-Saxon Chronicle, it raised no less than £167,000 during Ethelred's reign.[14]

When England became unified after Alfred's treaty with the Danish Guthrum, an arrangement, not dissimilar to that in Wessex described above, was in place throughout the country, although using different language: carrucates (in the Danelaw) or sulungs (in Kent) instead of hides; leets or wappentakes instead of hundreds.

Taxation in Norman and Angevin Times

Danegelds continued to be levied after the Norman Conquest. William I levied gelds frequently, possibly annually.[15] "What used to be paid to the Danes out of unspeakable terror," wrote Henry of Huntingdon (d. 1155), "we now pay to the King by custom". The last three gelds recorded, in the form of a carrucage (a land tax on a general basis), were levied in 1194 by Richard I, once by John, and again in 1220 by the regents for Henry III.

Danegelds had, however, come to bear so little relation to the distribution of cultivated land, and were limited by such extensive exemptions, that they had lost their national character. They looked only to cultivated land when the richest land was inside the towns in what was now developing into a trading nation. Once again the absence of reassessment to keep pace with change is apparent.

The Norman and early Angevin kings lived on the profits from their demesne lands, supplemented by rather arbitrary levies on the demesne called tallages. They also levied tallages upon the towns, and upon the Jews, as being under the immediate protection of the Crown and therefore part of the king's demesne. From the rest of English land, distributed by the Conqueror to his followers as tenants in freehold, the Crown received the recognized feudal dues - together with the customary incidents of tenure, many of them being commuted into money as time went by.

By the end of the twelfth century, largely through warfare and revolt, these revenues had become inadequate to provide for the Crown's expenditure. Danegeld was based on an out of date assessment centuries old. The

Domesday survey had never been updated. Scutage (shield money, a payment in lieu of knight-service), which had been the proper feudal method of paying for the wars of the Norman and Angevin kings, had been rendered almost useless by changing circumstances. The last survey had been in 1166:

> The survey of 1166 no longer represented the truth. A great vassal whose wide-flung manors, comprised, in parcels and fragments, a hundred knights' fees might himself owe the service of three or four knights. If he accompanied the king on an expedition and had his royal writ of scutage, he raised a sum which bore no relation at all to his expenses, or at any rate to the service he had rendered. Owing to the rise in prices and the higher cost of military equipment in horses and armour and maintenance, expenses were certainly growing, but as most of the charge was borne by the Crown, the king was increasingly reluctant to acquiesce in a financial arrangement which brought so little money into the exchequer ... The exchequer failed to turn scutage into a [regular] tax. By Edward III's time the implications of scutage had become unreal, its assessment was tiresome and intricate, its collection was very difficult. The knight's fee and all that it had meant sank to the level of an antiquarian survival.[16]

The essential feature of landholding up to this time had been that it provided the expenses of the court and the means of fulfilling most of the functions of central government. To meet particular emergencies danegelds were levied, and these had turned into a regular tax. Towards the end of the twelfth century, however, a general levy on movable goods had been several times resorted to, but always to meet a particular need: for example, for part payment of Richard I's enormous ransom (1193), for the administration of the Channel Islands, and for the recovery of Jerusalem (the 'Saladin Tithe') in 1188. The success of such a levy depended very much on the popularity of its objective.

The Thirteenth Century

In 1207, John succeeded in raising £60,000 in this way for the expenses of his French wars by levying a thirteenth (a shilling on the mark) on personal property and income. This compares with little more than £5,000 raised by danegeld, which was fast becoming obsolete, in Henry II's reign.[17] There were earlier precedents for taxing movable wealth; but the money so collected had not been for the benefit of the government, but for a definite charitable purpose - the crusade, for example. So great was the return when this thirteenth was raised in 1207 that a separate exchequer was created to deal with the proceeds. "The thirteenth of 1207 is the true forerunner of the tenths and fifteenths of later times".[18] These were termed subsidies. That title was, however, assumed in Tudor times by the subsidies granted by parliament, and these earlier aids to the king came to be called fifteenths and tenths.

The royal finances in John's reign were in a parlous state. He had the misfortune of following his elder brother who was exceedingly popular on account of his military exploits hence the case of collecting his unprecedentedly large ransom. Nicknamed Lackland, John was a younger son who did not inherit his father's personal estates. He too campaigned abroad, but with disastrous results, including the loss of Normandy, which was separated from England in 1204.

To meet the inevitable expenses of this situation "the elaborate fiscal and legal system of the country was turned into a merciless machine for extortion". This, together with his loss of England's French possessions and his unsuccessful quarrel with the Pope, led to strife between John and his barons, which ended in civil war, and an invasion by the French who occupied London and some of the shires.

In 1215, John and the barons reached the settlement recorded in Magna Carta, purporting to stop abuse by the King of his feudal dues and incidents of tenure. Scutage, a due which had assumed some of the features of a tax, was restricted to its former value. The feudal incidents of relief, wardship, and marriage were brought under control. So also Aids to the King. These provisions put an end to the expedients to which the King had resorted to make up for the changing value of money and the increasing costs of warfare and administration.

> The government at once set to work to give effect to the settlement. Evidently the king was trying to make the peace a reality. Not so the barons. Once in power they revealed the pettiness and arrogance common in men placed in positions beyond their capacity or their deserts ... It would appear that they did not intend to observe the Concord of Runnymede.[19]

The result was that in the decade following Magna

Carta the main burden of government expenses was shifted from land to personal property, and hence to the whole population except the very poorest, without any regard to their holding of land. How did this come about?

In January 1223 the regents for Henry II (aged nine when he came to the throne in 1216) ordered the sheriffs to inquire of juries in full shire court what the customs and liberties possessed by King John had been in 1215, when the Great Charter had restricted the finances of the Crown to its proper feudal dues. However this caused such alarm across the country that in April the order was withdrawn. Because of the desperate financial situation there had to be a settlement. A meeting with the barons was held in 1225 at which the Charters - the Great Charter and the Charter of the Forests - were confirmed and,

> The confirmation of 1225 contains the significant statement that "in return for the concession and gift of these liberties' the archbishops, bishops, abbots, priors, earls, barons, knights, free tenants, and *all people of the realm* had given a fifteenth of their movables" ... The taxation of 1225, as we can now see, meant the acceptance, without elaborate argument or clear intention, of the fact that the great council could, *in the name of the people of the realm*, grant a tax which every householder in the realm had to pay ... Now, in 1225, a great feudal gathering spoke for all and granted a non-feudal tax - a very special kind of tax which bore no relation to tenure or services - which was to be paid by all. (italics added)[20]

In contrast with feudal aids, taxation of this kind was new. Although it followed a deliberate and agreed determination to meet a particular emergency, it was later to become the normal way of increasing the royal revenue. It was levied only four times during King Henry's reign - 1225, 1232, 1237, 1269/70; each time to provide funds for a special purpose. But Edward I, who was constantly at war in France, or Wales or Scotland, was able to turn these financial expedients of Henry's reign into a normal way of raising revenue, and also to tap a source of revenue hitherto hardly touched: the growing foreign trade in wool and hides.[21] He also made up the deficit which remained by borrowing heavily abroad, and from the Jews at home. Having expelled the Jews in 1290, the ever-increasing wealth of the towns made it possible to borrow from rich merchants, chiefly in London.

Henceforward the revenue to support government came from diminishing feudal dues and incidents, and from customs, along with revenue provided by the Church, the history of which is complicated. The Norman and Angevin kings obtained income from sees and benefices which fell vacant; and made it very profitable by delaying new appointments. This practice was to stop after Magna Carta, but there were many breaches of the Charter. Winchester, for example, was left vacant for six years under Henry III. From time to time the clergy had been included in the early aids levied on movables, although at a lower rate than the laity. They also gave voluntary aids or gifts to the Crown, especially when a scutage was levied. Henry III and Edward I had good relations with the Pope, who contributed part of the papal taxes of the English clergy to support projects of which the Pope approved. The King got the best of the bargain because the papal officials made the assessments and collections, which were sometimes unpopular, and the king got the money. By the middle of the 13th century a clerical tenth came to be added regularly to the tenths and fifteenths collected from the laity. "The position of the clergy was clearly defined in 1307. Whenever lay subsidies were granted, the clergy were to pay on movables upon or issuing from lands acquired since 1291 or not taxed when clerical subsidies were levied".[22] The assessment and collection remained to be carried out by the clerical authorities until the reign of Henry VIII.

The total revenue from all these sources was, however, not enough. Borrowing had to make up the chronic deficit, and loans continued to swell into a major item of revenue until in 1694 the Bank of England was chartered to raise loans for the Crown, and (later) to be its banker. At the same time the inadequacy of the 'subsidies' led, after several attempts to re-fashion them, to the adoption of a foreign tax, the excise, 'a hateful tax levied upon commodities' (Dr Johnson), which has continued to this day, and is still continuing.

7

The Resort to National Debt

How had the remarkable change in public finance come about? The administrative mistakes are, with hindsight, not difficult to see. Behind them the root cause of the Crown's loss of revenue from land was a combination of greed and ignorance, together with administrative indolence and a certain amount of corruption.

The most obvious administrative failure lay in not keeping abreast of change. Although society was, compared with our own day, fairly static, it nevertheless changed dramatically over the years from an almost completely agriculturally based economy to a trading economy with a considerable international connection. At the same time commerce and finance were growing on an international scale. Moreover services in kind which characterized the early Saxon duties in return for tenure of land were being commuted into money payments. Villein services were widely and increasingly commuted into money rents in the twelfth century.[23] Yet rents did not take account of the falling value of money - largely due at that time to debasement of the coinage. Scutages redeemed for a capital payment were a disastrous mistake. When inflation is likely it is always unwise to allow the outright sale of an income bearing asset. The thirteenth century saw significant inflation. "Average prices were certainly rising from 1150 to 1300. Between the first half of the thirteenth and the first half of the fourteenth century, wheat rose about 50 per cent".[24] For a century or more after 1350 they were remarkably stable.[25] In the sixteenth century the imports of South American silver began sharply devaluing the currency, and prices nearly doubled during the first half of the century. By the decade 1551-60 the cost of living roughly measured by a 'basket' of foodstuffs had risen to nearly four times what it was fifty years back.[26]

Taxation (the danegeld) suffered in the same way. But more importantly the hide on which it was based, and the allocation of hides, seem never to have been reassessed. "It was already ancient in 1066,"[27] and therefore became increasingly unrealistic as time went on. Domesday, a remarkably speedy and efficient assessment of the nation's wealth, in some cases reflected the Anglo-Saxon hidage. It too was not brought up to date.

Knight Service commuted into scutage suffered from the same defects. By John's reign the wages of a knight had more than doubled. Scutage had not; and the fragmentation of large estates had made the return from a writ of scutage yield far less to the king than it did to the great barons. Scutage, properly levied to pay for war, resembled a tax, but was never turned into a regular scheme of taxation based on a fair and up-to-date assessment. The system "was riddled with incoherencies and practical difficulties".[28] In the face of resistance the exchequer after persistent efforts to collect scutage in the thirteenth century had to abandon its collection. Thus the general feudal levy and the grant of scutage, though they were not abolished, came to an end.[29] Funds for mercenary soldiers and military equipment had to be found elsewhere.

War was always an expensive business, and the country was very frequently at war. The cost was a burden which the exchequer found hard to bear. This appears to be the reason for the resort to subsidies, which, having originally been raised to meet special needs such as Richard I's ransom, had by Edward I's reign become the normal method of taxing. They were useful to the king because they brought in more than the obsolete danegeld and scutage. They were preferred by the magnates because in granting them "on behalf of the people" they were enabled to avoid their feudal dues as tenants-in-chief of the Crown. Subsidies pleased some because they could be avoided, at least in part, by the unscrupulous. The very poor were exempt. The sufferers were those close to poverty, whom the levy could make destitute, to the extent of having to give up their land.

Assessment of any tax on personal property is extremely difficult. Such property can be disguised or hidden. Much depends on the honesty of the payer. The opportunities for avoidance or evasion (to use modern terminology) are by no means equal. For that reason the yield of a subsidy varied according to the mood of the people. To support a popular cause the people were more willing to pay - Richard's enormous ransom, for example, or certain of Henry V's campaigns. It was, like income tax today, to some extent a voluntary tax. In 1290, for example, a fifteenth had raised £117,000. In 1297 a ninth (a much heavier fraction) raised only £34,419.[30]

Fourteen "searching"[31] assessments were made between

1275 and 1332 in order to raise various fractions. The fifteenths and tenths of 1334 raised £38,170, and from 1340 onwards the fractions used were always fifteenths and tenths: a tenth from the towns and the royal demesne lands, because they were already liable to tallage, and a (smaller) fifteenth from the shires.[32] The return on the tax had steadily fallen. Sir John Clapham comments (p176): "it was far too elaborate a system for the medieval, perhaps for any, administrator to work". Consequently in 1334 the assessment of that year was standardised so that each administrative unit had an agreed quota to collect in its district, so as to bring in a total of £38,170; the contribution of each shire, borough and township being assessed proportionately.[33] This took no account of fluctuations in wealth, "allowance, however, was made for decayed towns, and the yield of the tax steadily fell. Peers did not pay on their demesne land, and the landless did not contribute. When a fifteenth and tenth was voted the king knew that he would get about £30,000".[34] Professor McKisack further observes:

> Standardisation had the effect of turning the tax on movables into something resembling a land tax and the simplification thus obtained was not without its advantages. The standard valuation was far below the real value of a tenth and fifteenth and it was too rigid ... Later experiments with novel forms of direct taxation such as the tax on parishes proposed in 1371 and the poll taxes which followed it, were the natural result of dissatisfaction with subsidies based on assessments which had never been realistic and were fast becoming obsolete.[35]

These poll taxes were levied in 1377, 1379, and 1380. They were a disaster in the amount they realised, in their unpopularity, and above all in their unfairness when not graduated. They were a major cause of the so-called Peasants' Revolt led by Wat Tyler in 1381.

The decay of the fifteenths and tenths led in 1435 to a subsidy of a new kind. It was raised on income from land or goods: sixpence in the pound up to £100, a shilling on the remainder up to £200, and two shillings in the pound on total incomes above £400. This necessitated valuations both of land and of personal property. Theoretically at least it had the merit of being graduated according to ability to pay, and of the yield increasing as wealth increased, and the value of money fell. In practice, however, there were large-scale underpayments and evasions by the rich and privileged. Sabine[36] instances Anne, Dowager Countess of Stafford, assessed at £1,950, at least £500 short of her real income; also the Duke of York at £3,320 when his income was more than double. A number of other similar evasions are detailed by Professor Jacob.[37]

There was always an idea ingrained in English tradition that 'the king should live of his own'. In the eleventh and early twelfth centuries the king did indeed live of his own. Even as late as 1404 Henry IV was petitioned by his parliament that he should live of his own, and Edward IV in 1467 announced to parliament that he intended to "lyve upon my nowne, and not to charge my subjgettes but in grete and urgent cases".[38] Fortescue (Works I 463) estimated that Edward IV held possession of one fifth of the land of England. Although the Crown had lost a large part of its feudal dues, the Crown's revenue from feudal incidents was considerable. Where land fell vacant through death without heirs, or through conviction of felony, it escheated to the king who was entitled to the income from it until the land was regranted. It had become the practice to leave the land vacant for long periods for the sake of the income. Bishoprics, abbeys, and churches were left vacant for the same purpose. Magna Carta by prohibiting these abuses considerably reduced the revenue accruing to the Crown.

The Crown's revenue as supreme landlord both in feudal dues and incidents, including scutage which was supposed to pay for war, and the taxation of danegeld fell upon the rural landed interests. "The urban population, whose wealth and importance was steadily increasing were not comprehended in this scheme of finance."[39] The king had the right to tallage his demesne tenants, which included the royal boroughs. 'Aid' or 'gift' came to be used as a euphemism for this practice, since 'tallage' was a word associated with servitude. The levying of a tallage, the sale of a charter granting a jurisdiction, or of the right to hold a market, or a right to self-government, were the nominal methods of obtaining money from the towns. These had the defect of being grants for a capital payment which could not properly be repeated. Nevertheless various expedients were used to make the towns pay again and again: for example, by charging to have their charter confirmed, or renewed, or re-sealed by a new king, or exchanged for a slightly better charter. Yet this never produced the benefit of an assured regular income. The royal revenue was in effect extorted from the towns, and only their ever increasing prosperity made it possible for the towns to get the better of the bargain. This they undoubtedly did, as is shown by the large surplus of wealth the rich merchants lent at interest to the king after the expulsion (1290) of the Jews, who had been lending at a normal rate of 43 per cent, and occasionally at 60 per cent.[40]

The Jews had been treated abominably. Because they were under the protection of the kings, they were tallaged, and fined, and sold charters in such a manner that, bordering on ruin, many had already left the country at the beginning of the century in which they were expelled. There were some Christian moneylenders too, in spite of the prohibition of the Church. Richard I and John borrowed from Flemish and Italian merchants, and from the Knights Templar and the Hospitallers. From 1185 the Temple became a depository of royal treasure.

The pattern of royal revenue in the early years of Edward III's reign[41] suggests a return of about £30,000 from ordinary revenue; some £57,000 from fifteenths and tenths on all movable property; borrowings from the Bardi and other Italian financiers averaging between some £12,000 and £20,000 a year, with around £4,000 interest charges; taxes of a complicated nature on the wool trade which (optimistically) might raise £70,000 a year. This rough and ready calculation with figures not necessarily from the same year, is sufficient to show how taxes on production - there were other commodities under tax by this time - had reached more than double the return from feudal dues, with the deficit being made up by borrowing more than twice the amount of the ordinary revenue.

Edward was a warrior king. His victories at Sluys, Crecy, Poitiers, and Calais made him popular at home. Soldiers were now virtually all professionals paid by him, at wages which (when paid - which was infrequently) compared favourably with civilian earnings. Ransom money and booty made soldiering a profitable trade for all ranks when a campaign was successful, and brought prosperity to the country as a whole. After the Treaty of Calais (1360) Edward received at least £268,000 on account of ransoms of important prisoners. But the war had caused an immense rise in borrowing by the Crown. In 1338 Edward borrowed £100,000 in Brabant. In 1343 the Italian bankers - Peruzzi - went bankrupt with £77,000 owed them by Edward. An English company of merchants then agreed to pay him 10,000 marks a year and 1,000 marks every four weeks. The Bardi, to whom Edward owed at least £103,000, also collapsed in 1346. Another similar English company of merchants gave him an advance of £4,000 and a guarantee of £50,000 a year, on which they too went bankrupt.[42] These loans were usually secured by farming out the customs as security to the lenders.

The King borrowing from his English subjects had become one of the chief methods of making up the inadequacy of the revenue from obsolete feudal dues and taxation. The Crown was almost always in debt. Loans were thenceforward "an indispensable and normal part of the financial system of the Crown".[43] The treasury was empty when Henry IV seized the throne for the House of Lancaster in 1399.

At the beginning of the following century the Crown

was of necessity defaulting on its repayments. There were considerable delays of a bureaucratic kind. Creditors might get only partial repayment with a promise of the balance later. They might be asked to defer their demands. They might only get repayment at a discount. This arose in part from the funds available as security - chiefly the customs and the subsidies - being held in various centres throughout the country.[44] The fund of debt increased and incurred an ever increasing burden of interest.

Henry V was a strong and popular king whose demands usually succeeded in obtaining money enough for his wars in fifteenths and tenths from a compliant parliament, together with clerical tenths and aids from a willing priesthood. Successful campaigns demonstrated the voluntary element in this taxpaying, and also brought considerable profit, especially in ransoms.

When Henry VI came to the throne at the age of nine months in 1422, all this changed. During the next forty years England saw the loss of all Henry V's conquests except Calais (1453), the king's madness (1457), the outbreak of open hostilities between the families of Lancaster and York, and the chief battles of the Wars of the Roses. Henry was deposed and died in the Tower (1471), most probably murdered. The Yorkist king Edward IV died in 1473, and twelve-year-old Edward VI succeeded his father for two months. He too was probably murdered. Yet the Wars of the Roses did not significantly affect the working of the existing system of finance. Indeed there were considerable improvements made at the Exchequer, exemplifying once again the strength of the civil administration in times of turmoil, on which Professor

Keeton commented in respect of an earlier period (cf. Chapter 5, p.54 above). It showed itself 'proof against disruptive shocks', continuing with its job 'no matter whether kings or barons are in control'.

It was during Henry VI's reign that in 1435 the experiment already mentioned with a new kind of subsidy was made. In 1472 the Yorkist king Edward IV attempted unsuccessfully to raise a special tax of £51,000 assessed on goods and chattels in the first place, with power, if the whole sum was not obtained, to charge the deficiency on "lands and rents and other possessions of freehold". The order of preference as to the incidence of the tax is noteworthy. When the experiment failed the money was collected by the grant of fifteenths and tenths.[45]

Parliament was slow to grant funds, and the government staggered on close to bankruptcy by means of loans and a complicated system of credit management. The Treasury was continually unable to pay expenses out of revenue, and grants of subsidies were used, not to liquidate current expenditure, but as security for further borrowing. The customs remained as always the backbone of the system. When the defeat and death of Richard III at the battle of Bosworth in 1485 ended the contest for the crown in favour of the Tudors, Henry VII inherited a bankrupt realm.

By that time assessments had ceased to be made for the old subsidies (fifteenths and tenths). Their yield had gradually dropped. Neither goods nor land were valued. The amount expected from each county had become standardised, taking no account of fluctuations in individual wealth, and had become a standard revenue from which

£30,000 could be expected. This was a great mistake. It was a time of inflation, and it led to ever increasing borrowing. A strong king with parliament on his side could, and Henry VIII did, get parliament to pass Acts (1529 and 1544) repudiating certain of his debts altogether.

It was in Henry VIII's reign that a new type of subsidy evolved between 1513 and 1523 to become the established form of parliamentary grant under the Tudors and Stuarts. Incomes which were fixed and could be ascertained, as in the case of holders of office or landlords, were directly taxed at so much in the pound. Merchants, tenant farmers, professional men, and others whose incomes fluctuated, were assessed on the value of their movables. The old 'fifteenths and tenths', having become increasingly obsolete as money values declined, continued to be levied, sometimes with and sometimes without the new type of tax, which alone was now called 'the subsidy'. The last fifteenth and tenth on movables was granted in 1624.[46]

The essence of the Tudor subsidies is defined by Professor Dietz as "The alternate levy on either land or goods, newly assessed for each grant by royal officials and collected by them, with no exemption or remittances to favoured towns or localities".[47] Parliament appointed commissioners to supervise local officers who were to assess the tax each time it was granted, to raise a poll tax of fourpence and a graduated income tax which all had to pay.[48]

In practice, however, the Tudor subsidies failed of their purpose. The graduations and the basic fraction to be paid were varied several times. "In later grants the 'super taxes' of the Act of 1523 were stripped off, and wide limits of exemption were created, to include eventually more

80

than half of those who had paid under the Act of 1523."[49] The trouble was that people paid on either their land or their goods, but never on both. Land had to be valued - not difficult if done with the efficiency and speed of the Domesday survey. But goods were not susceptible to a proper valuation. They could be and were hidden or moved out of the district during the assessors' visit. 'Goods' included animals, household utensils, furniture, and clothing and so on beyond a certain minimum. A lucky escape was open to those who managed to persuade the assessors to tax them in a different district to that in which their main wealth lay. At first the assessment was taken on oath, but the oath was abandoned in 1566. The 'poor' had been omitted from the tax in the mid-15th century. Of the wealthy Raleigh said "our estates that be £30 or £40 in the Queen's books are not the hundredth part of our wealth". On the other hand, very poor men were repeatedly declared to be assessed to the full value of their property.[50] In a footnote Professor Dietz observes that Lord Treasurer Middlesex was rated at £150 in 1622; a paper in his own hand, dated October 11 1620, fixed his total wealth at £90,250.

The subsidy book soon came to be relied on more often than a proper examination. Lord North having just finished assessing half of his county in 1589 wrote to Lord Treasurer Burghley: "No man was assessed at but what was known to be worth in goods at least ten times what he was assessed at, and six times more in land, and many be 20 times, some 30, and some much more worth than they be set at, which the commissioner cannot without oath help".[51]

"Between 1540 and 1547 there were granted six fifteenths and tenths and three subsidies; the fifteenths and tenths remained constant at something over £29,000, but the yield of the subsidies reflected both the prosperity of the country and the results of inflation; that of 1540 produced over £94,000, that of 1543 about £183,000, that of 1545 nearly £200,000".[52] The men who paid the later Tudor subsidies were called 'subsidy men'.

> But, as often before, the valuation and revaluation of lands and goods proved too hard for what administrative machinery there was. Goods, even lands, ceased to be valued. A county was expected to yield so much and each 'subsidy man' was expected to pay his share. After 1540 - 1550 no attempt to hit the small man appears; subsidy men are the bigger fish. Even for them the tradition grew up that "men must not rise in the subsidy book although they rise in wealth.[53]
>
> In 1575 the Chancellor (Sir Walter Mildmay) was telling the Commons: "How favourable is the taxation of subsidies whereby far less cometh to the royal coffers than by the law is granted, a matter now known to be so usual that it is hard to be reformed.[54]

The subsidies have been referred to in some history books as land taxes. They were not. They were, as defined in Everyman's Encyclopedia, "Aids granted to the king, imposed not immediately on property, but on persons in respect of their reputed estates". They were grossly unfair, and were supportable only when they came to be paid mostly by the landed classes at a rate utterly insufficient to support the expenditure of the Crown. Like the fifteenths and tenths before them the 'subsidy' became stereotyped and fell steadily in value. Professor Dietz has calculated the yield of a subsidy of this type in 1621 as £72,500, in 1624 as £67,000, and in 1628 as about £55,000.[55] Bearing in mind that this was a time of considerable inflation, a comparison with the earlier figures quoted above demonstrates the failure of the Tudor subsidies.

8

Tudor Land Sales & Stuart Civil War

The reign of Henry VII is a watershed between the feudal and the modern method of raising public revenue. Henry Tudor tried his utmost, and with considerable success, to recapture the feudal dues and feudal incidents which had been lost to the Crown in the two preceding centuries. He enhanced the yield from the customs, which had been the mainstay of the Crown's non-feudal revenue since Edward I's time, by the simple expedient of encouraging imports, as well as other trade. He sought to avoid the expenditure on war by avoiding war so far as he possibly could. He avoided extravagance at court except when it was politically or diplomatically advantageous to impress foreign envoys or his own people. He made vigorous, profitable, and sometimes (some say often) unscrupulous use of fines to control his possible dynastic enemies and over-mighty subjects.

The most important of these five expedients is the resumption of revenue from land. Henry's immediate predecessors had resumed the control of a great deal of land which reverted to the Crown in the Wars of the Roses by death or attainder of the barons participating in the fighting. Henry was able to extend the process by resumption or confiscation of the estates of the Yorkists who had supported Richard at the battle of Bosworth, of the Cornish rebels, and of those who later supported the impostors Perkin Warbeck and Lambert Simnel, pretending as Yorkists to the throne. One of the former, Sir William Stanley, described as "the richest subject for value in the kingdom" was executed in 1495. Henry's first parliament enacted the resumption by the Crown of all lands of the Duchy which were in the hands of Edward IV (Yorkist) in the first year of his reign; all the estates of Henry VI (Lancastrian) held in right of the Crown, and of the Duchies of Lancaster and Cornwall, the Principality of Wales, and the Earldom of Chester. Henry was said to 'have in hand' a fifth of the land of England. He made the best of it by thoroughly reforming the stewardship and administration of his estates, concentrating control of their income in the Wardrobe under the Treasurer of the Chamber, and bringing their accounts under his personal scrutiny.

The result was startling. Henry VII was able to live 'of his own'. Moreover, after paying all the expenses of collection and administration and of the household and the Wardrobe, the excess left over from the Crown estates available for other purposes rose from about £2,500 at the beginning of his reign to £24,145 odd in 1504.[56]

This part of Henry's administration was popular. The idea that the king should live of his own was still ingrained in the English tradition. The corollary was that taxation was only to meet occasions of special emergency. Hence the Danegeld, and the subsidies in the years preceding Magna Carta to pay for a crusade or the king's ransom. Hence also the dislike of the subsidies old and new - a dislike resulting once or twice in revolt. Henry did observe the tradition of two centuries earlier of only asking parliament for subsidies when war or rebellion threatened.

His unpopularity arose in part from his policy of avoiding war. It was the warlike Richard I, Edward I, Edward III, and (later) Henry VIII who made themselves popular with the people by waging war - and their wars were all ultimately unsuccessful, even though magnificent victories (Crecy, Agincourt *et al.*) were won during the course of them. Strangely, however, Henry made a profit even out of the subsidies. The actual cost of his French war, of his expedition to Brittany, and of his wars against Scotland, and against the Cornish rebels, was less than the subsidies granted to him by parliament to meet those costs. He made a profit out of them of "a clear £100,000," besides reparations from the king of France yielding him a pension of £5,000, and nearly £15,000 in fines on the Cornishmen and Perkin's supporters.[57]

Henry used the procedure of post mortem inquisition on the land of anyone suspected of holding land from the Crown to ensure he did not miss the feudal incidents on marriage, wardship and escheat, and more importantly in order to establish recent record of who were tenants *in capite* of the Crown: "so that the king's title might be found of record, but that shall not only be for profit of the king but also of his heirs". For the same reason he insisted on heirs suing out livery of seisin, although the fines collected were minuscule.

The revenue from customs was enhanced by negotiating mercantile treaties with foreign governments, by comparatively small increases in the rates of old and new customs and tunnage and poundage, but more importantly by a new Book of Rates establishing the value of imports and exports on which duty was to be paid. Henry hired out his ships to traders, and advanced £87,000 capital to English and Italian merchants, interest free, on condition that they imported into England enough goods each year during the currency of the loan to pay certain amounts in custom dues. The average custom revenues for the first ten years of the reign were £32,951 per annum. They increased to average £40,132 during the rest of the reign.[58] This too was acceptable to the people, who innocently believed that it was the foreigners who paid.

Fines in feudal courts of law had always been a source of revenue to whoever had the jurisdiction. In Plantagenet times when the King took over jurisdiction, they had been described as the king's *magnum emolumentum*. In Elizabeth's day they had diminished to a mere £1,000.[59] Henry VII by contrast collected huge amounts[60] in fines from his richer subjects sometimes for genuine breaches of the law, sometimes on trumped-up charges. There is controversy about the doings of his law enforcement officers, Dudley and Empson, who were beheaded early in Henry VIII's reign 'for treason', amid general rejoicing. They may well have been innocent.

Forced loans or 'benevolences' were also a feature of Henry VII's financial dealings. One way and another he was the most successful English king in the management of public finance. At the beginning of his reign he was personally in considerable debt following his years of exile in Brittany. The treasury was empty. Even the crown jewels were in pawn, and had to be redeemed for his coronation. When he died he left at least £1,000,000, largely in jewels, plate, bonds and obligations. Some have estimated the total to be as high as £1,800,000.[61]

Whatever the figure was, his son Henry VIII soon dissipated it in lavish expenditure and ineffectual wars. After

> such exercises in regal grandeur as the Field of Cloth of Gold, there followed the period of Wolsey's supremacy. His oppressive taxation policy made enemies of those who finally caused his downfall. Thomas Cromwell retrieved the situation partly by more efficient management and partly by the expropriation and sale of the monastic lands. However in the end, to pursue his futile and ill-conducted wars, the king destroyed the financial independence of the Crown and undermined the prosperity of the country.[62]

When his younger daughter Elizabeth succeeded after Mary's short reign, the treasury was empty and the government was in debt, partly to foreign bankers, to the extent of over £266,000, and subject to 'biting' interest (Black 1959: 1). Elizabeth, although frugal in her ways, was so ill-provided that she was forced to sell land during her reign to the extent of £813,332. In so doing of course she was imprudently letting go the goose for the sake of a few of its eggs. She thereby lost for ever a regular revenue in rents.[63]

The Crown had been losing revenue to the Church long before that. It was the habit in medieval society to endow churches and monasteries with rich gifts of land.

> If a man gave land to a religious corporation the lord got a tenant who never died, was never under age, who could

never marry, who could never commit felony. It suffered none of those incidents [the feudal incidents] in the life of a natural man which were profitable to the feudal lord. Moreover, land held by religious corporations could not be so freely alienated as land held by individuals. For that reason it was said to have come into a dead hand (mortmain).[64]

To stop the loss of these valuable incidents of tenure was the object of the Statutes of Mortmain, the first of which was enacted in 1279. The Statute Quia Emptores (1290) was aimed at the same loss; but it had the more important additional effect of stopping subinfeudation, and so gradually bringing more and more tenants into direct holding from the Crown.

In selling crown lands Elizabeth was only following the policy of her father, who while adding considerably to the Crown's lands from the spoils of the dissolution of the monasteries, sold off some seven eighths of them to the new rich of his time. In the two short reigns of his infant son Edward VI and his daughter Mary, at least the best had been made of the royal demesne by reorganisation, by raising the rents to bring them up to date with steeply rising prices, and in 1558 by issuing a new book of Rates bringing up to date the custom valuations from their levels fixed in 1507.[65] This was once again the work of an efficient 'civil service', and considerably enhanced revenue from existing resources.

Much greater increases would have resulted in the yield of crown lands had all the property acquired remained in the possession of the crown. Elizabeth, James I, and Charles I followed the examples of their predecessors and sold vast tracts of their landed properties. According to a summary worked out in James' reign the land sales of Elizabeth involved property to the annual rental value of £24,808, the sale of which yielded £813,332 to the Crown ... Between 1603 and 1613 alone, James I sold lands worth £27,311 annually for £654,952. From his succession to 1635 Charles I parted with an approximately equal amount for £642,000.[66]

One can only guess how many billions that revenue would be today if it were still available to the Crown, and how much taxation it could have dispensed with over the intervening centuries.

These imprudent land sales were forced upon the Crown by sheer lack of financial backing from Parliament after the ruthless hand of the early Tudors was withdrawn. Henry VII's healthy fiscal legacy had been dissipated by Henry VIII. Elizabeth having inherited debt, left James Stuart with a backlog of debts which, together with the refusal by parliament to finance him, drove his able ministers to sell crown lands from time to time. Charles I completed the process of making it quite impossible for the king to 'live of his own'. The Crown was virtually left only with the duchies of Lancaster and Cornwall.[67]

Within three years of Charles' coronation in 1625 he was at loggerheads with Parliament over finance, and the country was on the verge of bankruptcy. Experiments with fiscal devices by the use of the royal prerogative, including 'ship money' and the sale of monopolies, were unsuccessful. Parliament in the Petition of Right (1628) claimed the sole power to tax. Coke, the Attorney-General and Chief Justice, is largely responsible for the doctrine, which persisted until the European Union of today, that Parliament was the supreme lawmaker.

In Stuart times the Commons consisted largely of freeholders. A contemporary Puritan diarist commenting in March 1627/8 on the House of Commons wrote: "I heard a lord estimate they were able to buy the upper house (his majesty only excepted) thrice over, notwithstanding there be of lords temporal to the number of 118. And what lord in England would be followed by so many freeholders as some of those are?"[68]

When the civil war broke out, Charles was supported by gifts from his wealthier supporters and by forced contributions from country districts. Parliament had London solidly behind it, and paid for the war by raising loans and subsidies assessed on property together with fines on vanquished royalist supporters. The party with the longest purse won the war.

During the Commonwealth and Protectorate, Cromwell depended for finance as usual on the customs, the revenue from which was buoyant especially after a restructuring of its administration; and a new way of collecting taxes on income: the Monthly Assessment. Parliament simply fixed the amount to be contributed by the various districts throughout the country, leaving it to local commissioners to raise the tax after inquiring into the resources of the local inhabitants. There was no uniformity in the assessments, there was a good deal of dishonest favour shown, and central control was extremely weak. "The result was that the easiest way out was taken and the tax became for the most part a stereotyped tax on land, where even the valuations of land were out of date, and personal incomes were either under-assessed or omitted altogether."[69] This repeats yet again the story of the fifteenths and tenths, and of the Tudor subsidies.

In 1643 during the civil war, on Pym's motion, the hateful tax called excise was introduced. It was a foreign tax with a foreign (French and Dutch) name. It was "a duty charged on home goods, either in the process of their manufacture or before their sale to the home consumer. Beginning with ale, beer, cider and perry, it soon spread to salt and butcher's meat. By 1645 hats, starch, copper, and many other goods were added. [It] continued throughout the interregnum - the main contribution coming from brewer's beer, not home-brewed, aided by low duties on salt and soap and some other commodities".[70] Dr Johnson described excise as "a hateful tax levied upon commodities". It plainly fell hardest on the poor.

At the Restoration in 1660, parliament when abolishing the feudal incidents perpetuated the excise on alcoholic liquors, and gave the Crown 'hearth-money' - two shillings on every hearth except the poorest. This was so unpopular that it was dropped in 1689 and replaced six years later by the window-tax, which was less burdensome to the cottagers.

> The excise was extended to houses (1696), to hackney carriages (1694), to hawkers (1697), to burials, births and marriages (1695), to bachelors, (1695); stamp duties were imposed on legal deeds and instruments and on law proceedings (1694). A hearth-tax was imposed in 1662, and a window-tax in 1747. The increase in the duties on

wines and spirits, tobacco, and tea led inevitably to smuggling on a very large scale and, in the eighteenth century, to widespread corruption among the officers of the customs and excise.[71]

After the 'glorious revolution' of 1688 the expensive foreign wars of William and Mary were largely financed by loans, the interest on which was charged on the excise as well as on other taxes.

> Ordinary articles of consumption were found easier to tax. One after another they were made to contribute ... malt and hops as well as beer; salt and soap and leather and coal and paper and candles. By 1715 the excise yielded £2,300,000, the customs £1,700,000 out of a total national revenue of £5,500,000 ... The balance came mainly from what had come to be called the Land Tax ... Originally called an 'Aid', it was meant, like the Tudor subsidy, to hit wealth in general - a shilling (later four shillings) in the pound on yearly income from lands and houses; from salaries; on income from merchandise, and goods generally on the assumption that they yielded six per cent on their capital value.
>
> Once again administrative difficulties proved too great. By 1698 the tax had become an 'apportioned' tax: each county was told to raise a certain share of the £500,000 or thereabouts which the tax was expected to produce, whether that meant a shilling in the pound of the residents' income or not. In effect this 'Aid' became the Land Tax that it was called; and although now and then the taxpaying capacity of townsmen was tapped a little, the squires' view that they and not the 'monied interest' paid it was not far wrong.[72]

It is thus simply a version of the subsidy which to be effective needed a widespread assessment of the value of personal property as well as of land. In effect the square-footage of land that had disappeared under buildings far exceeded in value the broad acres of the countryman. The money was in the towns and cities and most of all in London. No proper provision was made to get at it, with the result that the government had to borrow at interest the money which its lenders should have paid in tax. In 1798 Pitt made the 'land tax' redeemable by purchase. The Finance Act of 1949 provided for its compulsory redemption over a period of years.

The precise wording of the so-called 'Land Tax' (William and Mary 1692 Cap. 1) was: "Persons ... having an estate in ready monies ... or in any debts whatsoever owing to them, within this Realm or without, or having any estate in Goods, Wares, Merchandise, or other chattels or personal estate, within this Realm or without, belonging to or in trust for them ... [bad debts excepted] ... shall yield and pay 24 shillings in £100 ..." There followed taxes on salaries other than those of soldiers and sailors, and finally on "manors, tenements, profits and hereditaments" four shillings in the pound. This was certainly not a Land Tax. It was simply that the portion of the tax which was levied upon rents was the only part that was viable. Unlike the rest of the Act, this part lasted intact for over a century, but because it was never reassessed, had to be gradually abolished during the following half-century.

9

A Plague of Beggars
in Merrie England

In the 11th century the royal revenue consisted of the sums brought into the exchequer by the sheriffs in rents and profits from the forests and royal demesne lands, the feudal dues and incidents of tenure from other lands, the receipts from justice, and the tolls, and tribute from the towns. These provided the funds to support central government in peacetime. The King lived 'of his own'. Local government was carried on by lesser landholders at different levels, always supported by the services or produce of the land due to them - what we should today call 'rent' from their sub-tenants. The unit of land division was the tenement of a normal peasant, the holding which supported a ceorl and his household. A large house in the district formed a centre to which rents and taxes in kind or money were brought; hence 'the manor'. "Responsibility for payment of the King's *feorm*, for service in the *fyrd*, and all other public burdens was distributed over the country in terms of these peasant tenements."[73]

Taxation was considered necessary only for special expenditure, as in war, or rebellion. The important tax was Danegeld, a general land tax based on the hide of land.

This was a state of affairs where every free man provided by his labour and/or his wealth for the requirements of a homogeneous, society. The requirements were simple: Defence, Justice, and Administration by officers of the Crown. Defence was provided by thegns and knights who held their land in return for military service, and by all other able-bodied freemen because their landholding obliged them to serve in the *fyrd* when called upon. In Norman times the call-out of the *fyrd* was fast becoming obsolete, and knight service as a feudal due from military tenure was in the twelfth century being replaced by payment of scutage almost as if it were a tax. It was of course a commuted feudal due. In the thirteenth century the 'general levy' and the feudal levy existed simultaneously. Henry VII won the Battle of Stoke (1487) with a levy of Northerners - the royal host arrayed in three customary 'battles'. In the 16th century they became the 'trained bands', and in the 17th the 'militia'. But the customary period of two months' service in the year, and only within the realm, had long since compelled the kings to employ professional soldiers. For a time, which was remarkably short, these were paid for by scutage rendered in lieu of service by the knights. However, scutage had fallen into disuse long before its formal abolition in 1660. It had simply become useless in the changing circumstances of inflation, rising costs, and greater sophistication of warfare, and wars in far-off lands.

Taxation and borrowing then became the expedients to which the king was driven in order to pay for the defence of the realm. The injustice of it lay in the now 'redundant' military tenants continuing to receive their rents while passing little or nothing on to the Crown in place of their former service. The public rents of monastic lands too passed into private hands in Henry VIII's reign. It was the unwillingness of the feudal lords to relinquish any part of their land revenue after they had been released from their corresponding duties to the Crown which compelled the King to tax and to borrow. The barons were too strong for him, and the people had no say in the matter.

Justice in the 11th century was provided centrally or on circuit by the king in person and locally in manor court, court leet, court baron, or court customary, by the lord from whom land in the locality was held. The sanctions were economic, and to hold a jurisdiction was a lucrative business. A mirror of the structure of central government was thus repeated at lower levels to provide local government and its financial support.

Administration was supported, as indicated earlier, by money or service from landholders. Local taxes were few. But with the growth of professionals, both military and civil, who had to be paid salaries, the king was forced to rely on taxes (in origin 'aids'), and if parliament refused these, on borrowing. Because of his weakness in the face of the barons there was no other way that he could replace the revenue he formerly obtained through them from his people as tenants or sub-tenants of land.

Over the next 900 years the first notable change was the transfer of power to the central government. Judges were sent out on circuit in the King's name, and they gradually took over civil and criminal litigation from the local courts. They were preferred for their greater efficiency and their greater impartiality. Armed forces were now hired as mercenaries by the King, and in consequence the barons, quit of their feudal dues, and less bound to the king, became fractious. In the reigns of kings such as Stephen, John, Edward II, Richard II, and during nearly a century of rivalry between claimants to the throne after 1399 and in the Wars of the Roses of the 15th century, they raised local armies of their own and fought local wars. They were strong enough during this time to protect their lands from any updating of scutage. They forced John to grant Magna Carta, clause 16 of which (in one of the versions) precluded extraordinary scutage or aids being imposed unless by common consent of Council - in effect the barons themselves. 'Extraordinary' meant beyond what had always been charged, and completely ignored changing values and changing needs.

It was this that enabled them to take advantage of Henry III's minority to prescribe on behalf of "all people of the realm" a fifteenth of the movables, of all the people as an aid to the King on a special occasion. They thus made the general populace responsible for the revenue they themselves should have been providing. From that time onwards the barons only bore the burden of feudal incidents (not dues) in return for their land. The burden was heavy, especially because the King abused their use, as far as he dared, to raise money. Henry VII was a master of the art. But they were no substitute for the lost feudal dues. The chief incidents of tenure were not abolished until the Statute of Tenures 1660, which also converted knight service into socage.

The tax on movables, stabilised at fifteenths and tenths together with an 'aid' from the clergy, soon became a fairly regular means of taxing, which replaced the obsolete Danegeld. Fifteenths and tenths in their turn became obsolete, and were replaced by the Tudor 'aids' called subsidies, which taxed incomes. If the incomes were not fixed ascertainable sums, they were to be calculated from an assessment of either the subject's personal property or his land. Each of these three expedients to raise tax became obsolete because reassessment ceased to be carried out. In so far as they were based on discovering the value of a man's personal property, which in the Tudor subsidies included plate, merchandise and household goods, assessment was soon discontinued. Opportunities to disguise or hide personal property were too many. The land being impossible to hide, its assessment continued for longer, and in some cases was the only part of the tax to survive. When based in part on ascertainable fixed incomes the unfairness of the subsidies was manifest. Since there was no accurate machinery for ascertaining fluctuating incomes, it was fixed incomes that substantially paid the tax.

The so-called Land Tax of 1692 went the same way as the subsidies: "as had happened so often, difficulties of taxing personal incomes were again too great and the tax became little more than a tax on the rent from land".[74] It was forgotten that the Acts were aimed at income and contained the above-mentioned provisions to assess it. "The fact that the tax became popularly known as a land tax was a confession of failure by the state to make personal property and incomes, as opposed to realty, pay their share."[75]

But social and economic changes always make

continuing re-assessments essential. Villages decayed through plague or dearth or emigration. Population increased in some parts, and decreased in other parts. Yet Danegeld was still being levied in the thirteenth century on assessments which were ancient at the time of the Conquest. The tenths and fifteenths on movables, the Tudor subsidies which replaced them, the 'Aid' which came to be called 'Land Tax', all degenerated into stereotyped sums of money allocated between districts, which the local officials had to raise as best they could; and they did not, perhaps could not, do so without succumbing to pressure, financial inducement, and favouritism.

The result was that the Crown was always short of money especially in wartime. The struggle which developed between King and Parliament, resulting ultimately in civil war in the 17th century, was largely fuelled by the pressing financial needs of the Crown and the unwillingness of Parliament to concede taxes. Parliaments were dominated by landowners who were willing only to grand aids or subsidies which fell upon all the people. Land was sacrosanct. That these policies drove large numbers into poverty because they had no land, had to be dealt with by Poor Relief. This gave a somewhat grudging assistance, which did not develop into a reasonable level of assistance until the 20th century.

Having lost the dues payable by the barons, and having insufficient Aids from parliament, the Crown was saved from insolvency chiefly by the revenue obtained from the customs. Their origin is obscure; but they came into prominence when Edward I returned from a foreign war in desperate need of money. In 1275 Parliament granted him the great and small customs. Edward III was able to add the subsidies of tunnage and poundage, and of wool, wool fells and leather. Henceforward these customs along with many later additions became the mainstay of Government revenue, and remained so until overtaken by the hated excise instituted during the Commonwealth. When customs and excise were consolidated by an Act of 1787, there were no less than 3,000 dutiable articles, with the receipts from excise slightly exceeding those from customs.[76]

Whenever money was not available the Kings had to resort to borrowing, and from at least the twelfth century borrowing continually increased until debt became a mainstay of public expenditure, and the Bank of England was founded to take it over.

As another shift to raise more money, the Crown resorted to selling Crown lands. The later Tudors reduced not only much of their demesne land, but sold off most of the confiscated monastic lands. The high prices realised were a short-lived blessing. Speculators in those inflationary times were soon re-selling at much higher prices, and of course the rents were permanently lost as revenue to the Crown.

Land prices, whilst continually fluctuating, have over the long term always steadily risen ever since. Relieved of their duties in service or rent, head-tenants were increasingly able to use their land as a means of making money, buying and selling it just as goods and chattels were sold. This was because during all this time the Courts, aided from time to time by Parliament, were making the alienation of land easier. A tenant of land owed his lord feudal incidents and dues. He could not, therefore, alienate his land without his lord's licence. A tenant also had a duty to his heirs, and if he did alienate his land it could only be for his own lifetime. This latter rule only lasted until early in the thirteenth century; but for the protection of heirs it remained the rule that devises of land by Will were not permitted. These rules were more important and lasted longer in the case of tenants in chief of the King. "Such dignified persons as earls, barons, or tenants by grand serjeanty, were expected to fill very public positions and to perform very onerous duties."[77] Mesne tenants, however, following the statute Quia Emptores (1290), were allowed to alienate their land so long as the purchaser held the lands thereafter from the seller's lord on the same conditions as the seller had done. As already explained this gradually brought more and more tenants into direct relationship with the Crown as their intermediate overlord.

It is not difficult to see that the restrictions on alienating land brought stability to families and to society as a whole. But, as in our own day, stability did not suit the restless commercial thrusting of later centuries. Law usually follows public opinion, although its conservatism ensures that it does so only slowly. So the common law "came to regard the principle of freedom of alienation as a fundamental principle based upon public policy".[78] This certainly suited the commercial adventurers of late medieval England. It enabled them to enrich themselves by selling or renting out land freed from the duties to provide public revenue to the Crown formerly attached to it. Later still the economic and social revolution in

Elizabeth's reign prompted one historian to entitle it 'the Worship of Mammon'.[79]

> (p. 261) Undoubtedly there was a land hunger in Elizabethan England. Not only were capitalists dabbling in real estate: the law courts were busy from one end of the country to the other with claims arising out of land, or disputed succession to manors. Men flew to the law on the slightest provocation if they thought they could establish an advantage over their neighbours.

The result in terms of the dispossessed has been quoted already from the same source in Part I (pp. 35-36): "the great floating population of vagabonds that slept in haylofts, sheepcotes, or on doorsteps, spreading terror in the country and diseases in the towns", and forming part of "this merrie England".

Behind all these developments there runs, from Saxon times onwards, a thread of consistent thinking that the King must 'live of his own' except for aid from the nation in time of war. The King was of course the government, and remained so for many centuries. This thread runs through the continuing struggle between King and Parliament from the thirteenth century onwards. It was enshrined in English tradition almost as a doctrine. Two examples of its being publicly stated in the fifteenth century have already been given. In addition, Professor Dietz quotes Sir John Fortescue (Lord Chief Justice 1442) that only when there fell "a case overmuch exorbitant" for the suppression of rebellion, the defence of the realm to repel invasion and the safeguarding of the seas, was it thought right and necessary that the people should be taxed.[80] He points out that the 19th century historian Lord Acton would have us seek the baser motives, the special self-interest of the richer freeholders and gentry of the country and the burgesses of the towns who were precisely the persons who paid the fifteenths and tenths. In any case the tradition underlies the history of the struggle between the Kings and their barons until the Wars of the Roses so weakened the barons both politically and financially that the Tudor Kings were able to achieve royal supremacy. In the Tudor-Stuart period, Professor Dietz discerns the compulsion of "the traditions of fiscal policy, that the king must live of his own except for aid from the nation in time of war" (Introduction to Vol. I ix). It was echoed in the invariable preambles to William III's mis-named 'Land Tax'. They were 'Aids' declared to be "for the purpose of carrying on a vigorous war against France".

In England traditions often die hard, and this idea was probably only erased from public consciousness by the dire necessities of the First World War. It may, however, still underlie the modern legal principle that "the subject is entitled so to arrange his affairs as not to attract taxes so far as he legitimately can do". This is the bane of the Inland Revenue, and has led to a system that "is administered by an army of government servants and monitored on behalf of the taxpayer by a parallel number of legal and accountancy experts.[81] In 1993 it was estimated that the untaxed 'black economy' was worth between £36 and £48 billions.

Render unto Caesar...
Sir William Holdsworth[82] remarks that

all through its history, the importance of the land law has caused it to be influenced by all those social, political, and economic ideas which make up the public opinion of any given period ... and consequently, the rules relating to it are derived from many different periods in its history, and have been evolved under the influence of ideas which come from all those different periods.

Public opinion is subject to change. In the formative years of our law, the reciprocal rights and obligations of landlord and tenant were very much influenced by the dire need of security in troublous times. The tenant needed protection, the lord needed support so that he could govern, remain equipped and ready to fight, and fight whenever the necessity arose. Loyalty was essential, and was enshrined in tenants doing homage and fealty to their lord and rendering him service or money. Mesne tenants in chivalry paid escuage to their lord. Head tenants paid scutage to their lord the King. These were the tests of tenure by knight's service.[83] Unfortunately the head tenants (barons) were only too often in breach of these duties, not least when they openly rebelled, but for the most part in refusing to allow any change in the rate of scutage into which their service had been commuted. The remarkable thing is that their under-tenants remained so loyal, over the centuries of baronial infidelity to the monarch, in rendering service or payment to barons who did not render to Caesar the things that are Caesars.

It was not until the 20th century that the obligation to pay rent was seriously challenged by the lower degrees of tenant. Public opinion turned against landlords. The Rent

Restriction Acts, the Landlord and Tenant Acts, the Agricultural Holdings Acts, all put a curb on the rent which landlords of housing, shops, and farms, could demand. These Acts were a gift to lawyers, and had other undesirable side-effects in the troubles they were intended to cure. In particular they caused a shortage of houses, flats, shops and farms to let. Houses particularly had to be bought instead of rented. Leasehold enfranchisement created a new class of freeholders who were to pay no rent for their land after discharging the initial consideration for which they acquired the freehold. Recently a boom in house prices ended in disaster for borrowers on mortgage who were not content simply to buy a home, but who tried in addition to make money out of it. Public opinion had failed to appreciate that land-rent should not be bought and sold like chattels in order to make money.

Of the early English period Sir William says:

> In the primitive agricultural communities, which made up the Anglo-Saxon kingdoms, the land and the land law are so important, that almost all questions of Anglo-Saxon law and history seem ultimately to depend upon the original condition and gradual evolution of modes of cultivation, land measurement, and landowning.[84]

The difficulty we face today is that so much of our land has disappeared into oblivion under buildings where the more sophisticated modes of production - industrial, trading, commercial, and financial - have made the land more richly productive of wealth than any agricultural community could achieve. The value of such land has been immensely enhanced. Moreover the very word "land" tends to be taken as referring only to rural land and unused or waste urban land. Consequently in everyday thinking it is overlooked that an acre of waste land in the centre of a city is worth millions, or rather tens or even hundreds of millions of pounds, as compared with rural land worth a few thousand at most, or with rural waste land which has little or no value.

Economists from Adam Smith onwards have pointed out theoretically that, from the point of view of both the public and the individual, the optimum system of public finance is one that draws revenue from the rent of land. The history of the land law confirms this, and suggests that public revenue ultimately does come, however indirectly, out of the revenue of land. If it is not taken directly, then its collection by means of taxation causes all sorts of moral, social, and political difficulties amounting overall to injustice. Moreover the difficulties are compounded by attempts to rectify the injustice: for example, by returning as subsidies to industries on poor land such as farming, fishing, mining etc. some of the excessive tax collected from them; by paying relief to the poor who are unable to meet the taxation hidden in the price of the things they have to buy; and by maintaining at public expense those unable to find work. The yield of taxation then proving inadequate, the deficit has to be made up by borrowing at interest from those on richer land who have been undertaxed.

That direct taxation of the rental value of land, both rural and urban, is not at present contemplated amongst politicians seems to be the most remarkable defect in thinking shown up by any survey of our fiscal history. It is implied in the structure of the land law of today, and yet seems to go unnoticed, that ownership of the land of England is in the Crown, and that the users of the land are tenants, who in the course of history have been able to shed the duties of a tenant in respect of the owner (the Crown), whilst retaining the right to take rent from their under-tenants as if they were the owners. They have also with the acquiescence of parliament and the courts gradually acquired the legal right to sell their landholding without regard to their duties, and free of those duties. This occurred, and could only occur, before the establishment of fully representative government in the 19th and early 20th centuries. Few people prior to that time realised what was happening, even though they suffered the consequences. Those who did understand had no political power to protest effectively. "It was landowners who elected landowners to represent them in the House of Commons".[85] The Reform Acts of the 19th century enfranchised the landless, giving them power without responsibility. They remained landless whilst having the right to vote. What they needed was the opportunity to possess land which would qualify them to vote. By this time, however, any amount of land could be held without having to pay anything for the privilege beyond the initial consideration for acquiring it. That once paid, whether eight centuries before in Norman times or at any time since, there was nothing to lose by holding land under-used or indeed altogether idle for no matter how long. Taxation on production and consumption was replacing much of the Crown's lost rent. Under the burden of taxation, only the most enterprising - the entrepreneurs -

could contrive to buy their way into the land monopoly.

Taxation is an evil which should so far as possible be abolished except when the nation is faced with disaster such as war or rebellion. In normal times "the King should live of his own", which in present-day terms means Parliament taking the rent of land for public purposes and confining its expenditure to what the rent yields. Borrowing for necessary public works - roads, bridges, tunnels, airports etc. - would then be resorted to not so as to make up deficient ordinary revenue, but in order to profit from the rise in rent which the works create. The State in this way would receive revenue from any beneficial improvements it finances. Sensible public expenditure would be a public investment.

There are many lessons to be drawn from the history of the English land law and the public revenue. Some of the more relevant are:

(1) Payments to the Crown expressed as a fixed sum must be periodically updated to take account of the changing value of money. Scutage is an example. When the King belatedly tried to revise the rate of scutage, "the additional amount was simply not paid and the arrears [were] carried forward on the rolls".[86]

(2) Where tax is based on an assessment, there should be frequent re-assessments to take account of social and economic changes. The Rating system was abolished in 1989 because reassessment had been left too long, and had by that time become politically impossible

(3) The only assessments for taxation which were

successful were those based on land, but, again, only insofar as they were kept up to date.

(4) Almost every kind of tax except customs and excise enacted by parliament after the thirteenth century was at least in part based on personal property including wealth, and/or incomes. In each case evasion was rife, and the fluctuation in the yield of these taxes proclaims their dependence on the popularity or otherwise of the purpose for which they were raised. The opportunities for concealing money or personal effects are legion. They are to a certain extent always voluntary taxes.

(5) Taxes on incomes are never satisfactory because of the difficulty of making any accurate assessment, and because the opportunities for avoidance and evasion cannot satisfactorily be contained.

(6) Taxes on income are unfair in compelling those with a fixed, ascertainable, wage or salary to pay in full, so subsidising those who pay in part or not at-all. Today's PAYE is an example.

(7) The expense of assessing taxes on income or expenditure is wasteful to both government and taxpayer, and where industry is the payer, raises the costs of production. The modern income taxes, VAT, and 'payroll taxes' are current examples.

So little is land now regarded as the basis of life, that the language of taxation is also misleading. Taxes on people, in order to assess their income or wealth are called direct taxes. But wealth does not come from people directly. It comes from human industry applied to natural resources by people who live and work on land in village, town, or city; and who take advantage of the co-operation of the whole community, to the extent that it is available at their place of work. The wealth produced, or its proceeds when sold, is then distributed to all who have a claim to it. A direct tax would be one which falls upon the proceeds of production before they are distributed. Once distribution has taken place, any attempt to trace the recipients and tax them on their share is indirect taxation. History demonstrates that this kind of indirect taxation is bound to fail at least in part. Land is the nodal point where the factors of production meet. It is the proper point for the incidence of taxation. Freehold tenants of the Crown are loosely called 'owners'. What they own of course, is an estate in land of which they are freehold tenants, from whom no rent is collected. If they paid ground-rent, the whole community would to that extent be freed from taxation.

The feeling for land as the basis of life, if it has been overlooked by politicians, has not faded in popular estimation. It is a feeling soundly based on biological and territorial imperatives. Men and women all the world over are still prepared to die for their land - 'fatherland' or 'motherland' - or just "to gain a little patch of ground ... even for an eggshell" (Hamlet IV 4).

> Breathes there the man with soul so dead
> Who never to himself hath said
> This is my own, my native land?
> (Walter Scott)

The astonishing thing is that this spirit should have

survived in the landless pressed men who fought at
Trafalgar, and the common soldiers and sailors of the two
World Wars, few of whom were in a position to echo
Pope's praise of self-sufficiency:

> Happy the man whose wish and care
> A few paternal acres bound,
> Content to breathe his native air,
> In his own ground.
> (Pope)

Self-sufficiency was the victim sacrificed by taxation
when the Crown lost its rents.

PART III

Land-rent & Social Justice

10

A Basis for New Laws

In the course of the last hundred years many attempts have been made to explain the sharing of land, and to legislate for its implementation. Rather less in the public eye have been the attempts to explain that the natural revenue of any nation is the rent of the land they occupy. A formula is required which is relevant to modern conditions. It needs to look to a future in which institutional and fiscal arrangements can liberate people to achieve their fullest potential no matter what the wonderfully worded constitutions they live under may claim about liberty of the individual. Constitutions proclaim high-sounding human rights such as liberty, fraternity, and equality; justice and domestic tranquillity; and so on. But almost everywhere, and certainly in England, freedom is, for the majority of people, freedom to find a master whom they can serve for a wage or salary, and a landlord from whom they can rent or buy a dwelling place. Such is the power of land monopoly. Winston Churchill understood it:

> Land differs from all other forms of property. It is quite true that the land monopoly is not the only monopoly which exists, but it is the greatest of monopolies - it is a perpetual

monopoly, and it is the mother of all other forms of monopoly. It is quite true that unearned increments in land are not the only form of unearned or undeserved profit which individuals are able to secure, but it is the principal form of unearned increment which are not merely not beneficial, but which are positively detrimental to the general public. Land, which is a necessity of human existence, which is the original source of all wealth, which is strictly limited in extent, which is fixed in geographical position - land, I say, differs from all other forms of property in these primary and fundamental conditions.[1]

Those who fail to find a master, or who cannot afford the rent or price required by a landlord, have to be supported by charity, or as is usual in present day Europe, by the state. This has been glossed over by the great modern tendency to use politically correct euphemisms to conceal the truth. *Poor Relief* is now called W*elfare* or S*ocial Security,* implying that poverty has been abolished. Fifty years ago the standard legal textbook was accurately entitled *The Law of Master and Servant.* Today the truth is glossed by the title *Employment Law* in order to make us believe there are no servants and no masters. But there is no disguising the fact that there are "ghettos" which respectable people are not prepared to enter; and that middle class housing developments are usually built at a distance from the local authority's council estates.

Only Parliament has the power to implement the changes necessary to make the collection of the public revenue conform with natural law. One thing can be done at once to facilitate the collection of land rents. Parliament should speed up the work of registering title to land. At present about a third of the 22 million land titles in England and Wales are still unregistered. Compulsory registration of the remainder (including, ironically, the Land Registry itself in Lincoln's Inn Fields) needs to be hastened. If the titleholder of unregistered land cannot be traced, then the Crown should be given power, after due advertisement as prescribed by Land Registration Rules, to take possession of that land, and if no claimant to the land gives notice of his claim within a prescribed period of time, to retain it in permanent possession of the Crown.

Further legislation requires a re-examination of current conceptions of property, and its protection by the state: from which would follow an understanding of the natural laws of public revenue. The whole tenor of the history set out in Part II above shows how parliamentary taxation to provide revenue for the Crown has for the last five or six hundred years been based almost entirely upon expediency. Whatever was thought could bear tax, was taxed. The only arguable exceptions are the so-called "health taxes" of recent times to discourage smoking, drinking, gambling, the use of leaded petrol and so on. But all the Crown's revenues should be based on principles of Natural Law which positive law should strive to follow. People should pay to society the value of what they receive from society, which is reflected in the value of the land they occupy. To allow that value to be bought and sold between private individuals is morally wrong. Land is, by natural law, the common property of the community.

These and other principles of natural law were incorporated into a remarkable Bill introduced in the

Legislative Assembly of the Queensland Parliament in 1890 when the distinguished Australian lawyer, Sir Samuel Griffith, was Prime Minister. The Bill was entitled *The Elementary Property Law of Queensland*. The preamble reads: "Whereas it is essential to the good order of every State and the welfare of the people, that all persons should have and enjoy the fruits of their own labour, and to this end it is expedient to declare the natural laws governing the acquisition of private property: be it declared and enacted by the Queen's Most Excellent Majesty" ... etc. "The principle of the Bill," Sir Samuel told Parliament, "is this: That men's remuneration shall be in proportion to the work they do - that is to say, that the products of human labour shall be divided amongst the labourers in proportion to their contribution to the product. That is the main principle of the Bill, and I believe that only by adopting that principle shall we get over the terrible inequalities that exist in the world."[2]

Clause 15, for example, states that "the right to take advantage of natural forces belongs equally to all members of the community"; Clause 16, that "Land is, by natural law, the common property of the community". Clauses 22 and 24 are to the effect that the net products of labour belong to the persons (defined very widely) who are concerned in the production; and when for the purposes of production land is required, the person who receives rent [for it] is not, by reason only of his permission to use the land, concerned in the production, and is therefore not entitled, by reason only of such permission, to any share of the net products.

The Queensland Bill never passed into Law. Perhaps it

was never meant to. When the States were drawn together to form the Commonwealth in 1901, Griffith became the first Chief Justice presiding over the High Court of Australia. After his retirement in 1919 he published an article[3] urging the abolition of what he termed the 'Mastery Rule', whereby the great majority has to obey the command of a small minority. He concluded that if the community at large could be taught to regard the principles of Natural Law, as set out in the Elementary Property Law, as axiomatic, in the same way as they regarded many other rules of right and wrong, the world might at length attain to a 'Fraternity Rule', which would be no more than Christ's command to love thy neighbour as thyself, than which there is no truer democracy. The Bill emanates from a country which has graced the Common Law with a number of legal luminaries, both judicial and academic, and repays study by anyone attempting to follow Natural Law in drafting a statute relating to land tenure. Any radical politician would also find it instructive. A copy of the Bill is annexed in the Appendix (p. 141).

In England at the beginning of the 20th century the land monopoly aroused such public interest that a Liberal government attempted to introduce legislation to bring it to an end. This provoked opposition from the House of Lords that led to a constitutional crisis as a result of which the Lords lost the right of vetoing money Bills. The legislation was finally passed as the Finance Act 1910, but it contained so many complications and concessions, and was so limited in the revenue it might raise that the administration of its provisions proceeded at a slow pace, and was overtaken by the dire emergencies of the first

World War. It was repealed soon after the war ended. The only lasting legacy from this attempt are the speeches of Lloyd George as Chancellor and Winston Churchill as President of the Board of Trade describing and explaining land monopoly.

An attempt to tax land values was included in Philip Snowden's Budget of 1931. But, although passed into law, it was suspended on the formation of a National Government to meet the troubles of the great depression, and was later repealed.

In 1939 the London County Council attempted to introduce a private Bill to base local rates in London on the value of sites. This is the best drafted of the various attempts that have been made to collect ground rent from urban land. But it was rejected as being a taxation measure requiring a Public and not a Private Bill. This was unfortunate, because if passed into law it would have provided a rewarding and instructive pilot scheme on which to base national legislation.

Legislative measures since the Second World War to obtain for the public purse the benefits springing from the development of land can only be described as a disaster. These provisions were contained in the Town and Country Planning Act 1947, the Land Commission Act 1967, the Community Land Act 1975, and the Development Land Tax Act 1976. They were marred by being mixed up with complicated town planning provisions, by vacillating between contradictory meanings of the word 'land', and by diversion from the simple intention of the legislation in order to suppress speculators, and to tax the wealthy. These Acts have been criticized succinctly, forcibly and with commendable clarity by Mr. V. H. Blundell.[4] He summarizes the objects: making more land available for use, bringing down land prices, curbing speculative profits arising from the implementation of regional and national plans, enabling local authorities to acquire land cheaply, and collecting for the community those land values which were created by the community. He then sets out concisely a variety of reasons why,

> Although the Acts were eventually abolished by political action, this was no more than the *coup de grace* to legislation which was manifestly not achieving the objects for which it was originally introduced.

It needs no argument that our present-day system of taxation is unsatisfactory. Too much is taken in tax. Too much is avoided by those who can afford the assistance of highly paid lawyers and tax consultants. Too much is lost through evasion, through fraud, and through the high cost of collection. The cost in book-keeping and accountancy which the system thrusts upon the taxpayer is a grievous burden, especially in the calculation of VAT on sales, and of PAYE on wages and salaries.

Legislation to collect the Crown's lost ground-rent is most desirable. It needs to be simple. The legislation must hold fast to principle, and make no exceptions in favour of any vested interest. There must be no diversion from the object of the Act, which will be to resume collecting land-rent for the Crown. Any extraneous desire to 'soak the rich', or to relieve the poor, or to thwart speculators, has to be put aside. The sole aim is to achieve justice. The legislation must not get mixed up with town planning, except to lay down that in assessing land-rent the planning restrictions in force at the time of assessment shall be assumed to be perpetual.

It has to be borne constantly in mind that the announcement of any change in policy at central or local level changes the value of all land that is affected by it. As the policy is carried out so the value goes on changing either up or down according to betterment or detriment of the land affected. It is wrong to allow those detrimentally affected by the changes, and those unjustly enriched by them, to continue in that state for a moment longer than is necessary. It is therefore most important that reassessment of the proper rent is made at intervals frequent enough to keep pace with today's swiftly changing world. With modern technology, computers in particular, this could after a year or two be a reassessment every year. After all, the material for Domesday book was compiled without any such aids within twelve months of the Christmas Council of 1085 when William ordered it.

11

Geocleronomy - A New Approach

The time has come for a new multi-disciplinary approach to the study of Man and his relationship with land. It is not just a matter of economics. Anthropology, biology, psychology, sociology, and above all law and theology should also be concerned. Positive law, defined by Griffith as including all written laws enacted by a competent legislative authority, and all unwritten rules declared by the law of the state, needs to follow Natural Law. The writings of Locke (1632 -1704) and of Blackstone (*Commentaries*) are the nearest approach to a proper answer so far. But they are neglected in Britain, and only partially studied in the United States, where they had earlier dominated legal and constitutional thought.

The fundamental principles are rather obvious! Man is by nature bound to the dry surface of the earth, which the geographer calls 'land'. He may roam far and wide in mind or spirit, (without going out of my door, I can know the whole world, said Lao-Tse), but his physical body is "of the earth, earthy", and after death is committed earth to earth, ashes to ashes, dust to dust. It follows as a matter of *Natural Law* that throughout life his dwelling-house must be on the earth's dry surface, and he must get his living - his food, his drink, and all his other needs - from the resources of Nature which are available from the position he happens to occupy on 'land' in this its geographical sense. Any excursion by sea or air is bound to begin from dry land and end sooner or later in landfall. In primitive societies, if Man gathers the fruits of the earth, hunts animals, catches fish, or traps birds for his sustenance; or if, in his later development, he tills the ground, and excavates for the rich natural resources under the ground, *Natural Law* is inexorable: he has perforce to do all these things from his position on the dry surface of the earth. There is another resource that is easily overlooked. From his position on the earth's surface Man may take advantage of the benefits emanating from the society to which as a "social animal" by nature he belongs. Accordingly his closeness to markets, to centres of population, to transport services, to supplies of water, gas, electricity and the like, becomes more and more important as that society develops and elaborates.

Locke grasped this: "The great and chief end, therefore, of men's uniting into commonwealths, and putting themselves under governments, is the preservation of their property".[5] He went on to define two kinds of property, one the creation of individual people, the other the work of our divine author and the society He has created. That in fact makes three, as is to be expected because of the law of Trinity! Wealth is created in part by individuals, in part by natural resources, and in part by society. All three of these are of course created by God. The possession of land gives the landholder access to and control over the three kinds of property differentiated by Locke. The great question concerning property *rights* is - who has the *right* to each kind? Unfortunately Locke was diverted by his theory of labour-value from finding the answer. He concluded that by comparison with the value of labour the other two contributions were infinitesimal. The value of a city centre site today, however, in some cases worth over a hundred million pounds per acre, entirely refutes this.[6]

These elementary and indeed very obvious facts ought not to need stating. But they have unfortunately been lost sight of in modern man-made legal systems. There is, first of all, confusion between different definitions of 'land'. First, there is the legal definition, hallowed by Coke and Blackstone, to include everything *ab inferis usque ad caelos* - below and above the surface of the earth: in this sense 'land' includes buildings and other improvements. Secondly, 'land' is used in common speech to designate the country as opposed to the town: this omits the most lucrative location in any community, namely land on which houses, shops and offices stand. Thirdly, the economist takes 'land' to mean all the resources of nature available to the labour of Man, all the powers of the external world which he can use: this definition tends to obscure the huge assistance to production afforded by connection with other human beings whose co-operation can assist him. None of these definitions makes sense now. The legislation, national and international, controlling minerals, flying space, tunnelling, radio waves and so on makes nonsense of the legal definition. Overlooking the land underneath buildings has since the early middle ages bedevilled the sensible collection of the Crown's revenues. The immense superiority of land in the centre of a city compared with any rural location is almost entirely due to the proximity it affords to the markets of the world in which to obtain co-operation with the rest of mankind.

If 'land' is taken in the geographer's sense as the dry surface of the earth, then it is easy to see that a man's *position on land*, whether outside in the open or inside a building on whatever floor, determines the extent to which the free gifts of God are accessible to him - sunshine, wind, and rain; river, sea and sky; woods, flowers and natural fertility; mineral wealth of all kinds; indeed all animal, vegetable and mineral nature. It also determines how much use he can make of the co-operation of his fellow human beings. In the City of London, for example, a man engaged in certain types of work is in immediate touch with New York, Tokyo, or any other great market centre in which he wishes to deal. On a remote hillside, by contrast, even access to a local market town is beset by difficulties of time and space. There the advantages of nature are the predominant factor. In the city it is co-operation with others that matters most.

The benefits of Nature, and the advantages of being part of a community, fall upon mankind in vastly different degree depending on the precise position of the bit of land (in the geographical sense) that a man inhabits. Some will be very poor, and some very rich, unless adjustment is made for the advantages and disadvantages of their respective positions. The extremes are in fact not just 'very', but excessively, shockingly and indeed unjustly far apart. This is why in greater or less degree there are attempts at providing artificially for the poor and needy: an artificiality that leads to crippling systems of taxation and borrowing, public and private. For this purpose a morass of man-made law everywhere attempts to regulate direct and indirect taxation, social security, interest rates, prices, incomes, and all the fraud and other crime they engender. Moreover Town and Country Planning, the legislation for which takes up over a thousand pages of Halsbury's Statutes, adds to the tangle. It is extremely complicated. It is also very expensive to administer. Yet it is toothless when it comes to preventing the unjust enrichment which accrues to a successful applicant for planning permission.

We unfortunately live in an Unholy Trinity of taxation, poverty, and welfare. Taxation causes poverty because it falls hardest on the poor. Poverty necessitates Poor Relief, now euphemistically called Welfare. The funding of welfare increases taxation, which increases poverty, and so on in a vicious circle until escape is made by borrowing. But the escape is short-lived because interest on loans simply starts another unholy trinity of borrowing, interest payments, and either more borrowing or more taxation. That taxes press hardest upon the poor is illustrated by the incidence of indirect taxes. VAT is one example. Another is the price of bread on which there is no VAT. As with everything manufactured, the price of a loaf has to cover all taxes incurred during the process of production. The farmer who sows the seed and cultivates the crop, the miller who grinds the corn, the baker who makes it into a loaf, and the retailer selling it; each of these has to pass on to the next in line the fuel taxes, vehicle taxes, and VAT on machinery used in production and transport; as well as "payroll taxes" on labour - that is, the

deductions they have made from wages and salaries for
Pay As You Earn Income Tax and National Insurance
contributions. These the employer hands over to the
Inland Revenue. The workers never see the money. All
this accumulating taxation has to be passed up the line of
production so as to be included in the final price of the
loaf. To the rich it has no significance that a loaf carries
so much tax. To the poor it means a great deal, but it is
hidden from them. To the very poor it could mean under-
nourishment, or even perhaps starvation.

Natural Law proclaims that, in stark contrast to this
unholy muddle, to share land-benefit directly is simpler,
fairer, and less damaging to both givers and receivers. It
is not surprising to discover that "the universal moral law,
known by reason and confirmed by revelation, binding in
spite of our failure to observe it" (see the opening words
of Part I) carries this same truth. It is to be found in the
teaching of the scriptures. For Jews it is the Torah (the
Law) in the Old Testament. For Christians also it is the
Torah, which Christ said he had come to fulfil, "For verily
I say unto you, Till heaven and earth pass, one jot or one
tittle shall in no wise pass from the law, till all be fulfilled"
(Mt. 5: 18). We do well to study this Judaeo-Christian
revelation in both Testaments.

The essential references have been set out in Part I.
When God instructed Moses, and later on Joshua, to
divide the promised land equitably between the Israelite
families as their inheritance from Him, the word used in
the Septuagint is *klêronomeo*. This is a very important
word occurring often in the Old Testament. Its root *klêros*
is the 'lot' inscribed with one's name which is cast into a

receptacle whence the winner's name is drawn. Hence it comes to mean "that which is assigned by lot - an allotment of land to the citizens": hence again "any piece of land, farm or estate". Thus *klêronomeo* means "to receive one's share of an inheritance; to inherit".[7] In ancient societies dividing by lot was widely considered the fairest way to distribute what could not be precisely cut into equal pieces. Children do the same today, often through selection by nursery rhyming. *Klêros* is therefore a suitable word to imply equitable sharing.

Thus the means by which sharing of land might be achieved for the benefit of the community could well be called *geocleronomy*. This would be to adopt the very word that Christ used in the New Testament beatitudes to describe the Kingdom of Heaven in terms of the Old Testament scriptures, and declared the joy of the poor and oppressed (*praeis*) when they come into their inheritance of land (*Klêronomeo*), and the joy of "those who hunger and thirst for Justice; for they shall be satisfied". The meaning of *geocleronomy* is:

geo-,   'land' -
klero-, 'equitable sharing of inheritance' -
nomy-,   'the laws of'.

viz. "The laws governing the sharing of the inheritance of land".

It would be for the Churches to preach geocleronomy from the pulpit, taking as text the words of Christ: Blessed are they that hunger and thirst after Justice. It would be for the universities to establish chairs or faculties combining in 'geocleronomy' all the related social sciences to replace some of the discredited studies of the dismal science of economics. Under their influence Parliament could then understand the necessity for resuming the collection of the Crown's revenue as overlord of our heritage the land.

The Torah (Law) makes it clear that the nation's land is an *inheritance* from God which has to be shared equitably amongst the *families* of the nation. A nation is an aggregation of families. Accordingly the fifth commandment is: "Honour thy father and thy mother that thy days may be long in the land which the Lord thy God giveth thee". Sir Henry Maine pointed out that families, not individuals, were the units of ancient societies.[8] In modern society by contrast, the state has increasingly made the individual the unit with which it deals, over-riding the family to such an extent that there are children today seeking, with the help of social workers, legal remedies against their parents.

Today the land is bought and sold for profit, and the profits are sometimes vast. This is legitimate under man-made law, but it is in breach of divine law. The Lord had said to Moses in Mount Sinai:

> "The land shall not be sold for ever: for the land is mine; for ye are strangers and sojourners with me".[9]
> "This verse enunciates the basic principle upon which all these enactments rest. 'The earth is the Lord's' (Ps. 24: 1), and His people hold their lands in fee from Him. The ground itself, then, was not a proper object of sale, but only the result of man's labour on the ground."[10]

That land has to be divided fairly is understood as

Natural Law by aboriginal peoples. But the more separated they become from Nature, the more they forget the justice of land-division. When religion declines in modern society, Mammon is worshipped not least in the speculative buying and selling of the nation's inheritance. If the land has been monopolized into the hands of fewer than the whole population, then those left out have nowhere to live and nowhere to work. Having lost their inheritance they perish unless looked after, as they ultimately are in European countries, by charity or by taxation levied by the state. This degrading dependency on state support is no proper substitute for being given the opportunity to support their families by their own honest labour. But for that, land is necessary.

When Natural Law is forgotten by the educated, the plain man, even if he does not believe in God and has never heard of natural law, still has common sense with which to recognize that it is wrong for anyone to charge for access to 'God-given' natural resources; and that those who enjoy special benefits from the work of the community should pay for what they get. But if justice as prescribed by divine and natural law, and by common sense, is to be brought into effect today, much work is needed to be done. The physical division of land is impossible in developed countries. The diversity of its yield to those who work on it is so startling. A day's work in a few square feet of office on an upper storey in Lombard Street can earn thousands or even millions; while a whole year's work at the margin of society on an extensive acreage, may sometimes scarcely afford a living wage. It is therefore the difference in *yield* of land that has to be shared. There is no difficulty in this.

It is precisely measured by the market rent (i.e. the ground rent) of the land.

There is, however, another way - a much simpler way - of looking at all this, a way available to those having religious belief in no matter which of the world's religions. God created Man as a social being, and the emergence and growth of society was inevitable from the moment of Man's creation. The all-seeing and all-knowing Creator foresaw that man would, and intended that he should, combine in communities - the family, then the village, the town, the city of millions, and finally states of scores of millions with elaborate industries and complex organizations, needing revenue for a multitude of public purposes. He that made the world and placed man in it must have foreseen this ever increasing need for public revenues, and made provision for it. He must, therefore, have provided societies great and small with a natural revenue to be used for their common purposes. It is our duty to discover what this natural revenue is, and the duty of governments to ensure that the publicly created revenue goes into the public purse. If they allow it to be appropriated by individuals, then governments are driven to rely for revenue on taxation of all sorts and kinds levied on the product of labour: and this is a breach of the injunction 'Thou shalt not steal'. Many who only labour are driven into poverty; others while working grow rich by being so much better placed, while others grow rich without working, and those who cannot work are compelled to rely on the state to support them by further taxation.

References

PART I

1. 1610 8 Co. Rep. 1142.
2. Introduction, Sect. 2.
3. Cited in L.L. Blake, *Young People's Book of the Constitution,* London: Sherwood Press, 1982, p. 13.
4. Robert V. Andelson & James M. Dawsey, *Wasteland to Promised Land: Theology for a post-Marxist World,* London: Shepheard-Walwyn, 1992.
5. Luke 16: 19-20.
6. Luke 4: 18.
7. Robert Giffen, *Essays in Finance, 1879-1896,* Vol. 2, p. 393.
8. John Tanner. Bernard Shaw gives no further reference.
9. *Chambers' Encyclopaedia,* London: George Newnes, 1950, Vol. VII, p. 139.
10. *Cambridge History of the British Empire,* Cambridge: C.U.P., Vol. 7, p. 68.
11. Llewellyn Woodward, *The Age of Reform,* Oxford: O.U.P., p. 470.
12. A.L. Poole, *Domesday Book to Magna Carta,* Oxford: O.U.P., 1955, Vol. 3, p. 477.
13. Peter Ramsay, *Tudor Economic Problems,* London: Gollancz, 1972, p. 26.
14. John Clapham, *Concise Economic History of Britain,* Cambridge: C.U.P., 1949, p. 45.
15. G.M. Trevelyan, *History of England,* London: Longmans Green, 3rd Edit., 1945, p. 87.
16. Te Rangi Hiroa, Sir Peter Buck, *The Coming of the Maori,*

Christchurch N.Z.: Whitcombe and Tombs Ltd., 1966, p. 379.

17. *Ibid.*, p. 382.

18. *Chambers' Encyclopaedia, ubi sup.*, Vol. I, p. 137a.

19. Max Gluckman, *Politics, Law and Ritual in Tribal Society,* Oxford: Blackwell, 1967, p.37.

20. M.W. Stirling, *Indians of the Americas*, Washington D.C.: National Geographical Society, 1955, p. 55.

21. Henry Maine, *Ancient Law,* London: John Murray, 1906, pp. 136 ff.

22. *Chambers' Encyclopaedia, ubi sup.*,Vol. III, p. 614a.

23. Sir Frank Stenton, *Anglo-Saxon England,* Oxford: O.U.P., 3rd Edit., 1971, pp. 277-8.

24. *Ibid.*, p. 476.

25. Frederick Pollock and F.W. Maitland, *History of English Law,* Cambridge: C.U.P., 2nd Edit., 1923, Vol. I, p.48.

26. *Ibid.*, Vol. II, pp. 516-7.

27. *Ibid.,* p. 517.

28. Sir Maurice Powicke, *The Thirteenth Century*, Oxford: O.U.P., 3rd Edit., p. 367.

29. *Chambers' Encyclopaedia*, Vol. 11, p. 221a.

30. J.D. Mackie, *The Early Tudors*, Oxford: O.U.P., 1952, pp. 448-458.

31. J.B. Black, *The Reign of Elizabeth*, Oxford: O.U.P., 1959, p. 264.

32. *Ibid.*, p. 265.

33. Encyclopaedia Britannica: *Crime and Punishment*, p. 807.

34. J.L. & Barbara Hammond, *The Village Labourer,* London: Longmans Green, Vol. I, p. 3.

35. Quoted in Robert Bridges, *The Spirit of Man,* London: Longmans Green, 1916, No. 29.

PART II

1. Sir William Holdsworth, *Historical Introduction to the Land Law,* Oxford: O.U.P., 1927, p. 3.

2. III 314 E.

3. D.J. Hayton, *Megarry's Manual of Real Property,* London: Stevens, 1982, 6th Edit., p. 23.

4. Stenton Sir Frank, *Anglo-Saxon England,* Oxford: O.U.P., 3rd Edit., 1971, p. 680.

5. *Halsbury's Laws of England,* 4th Edit. Vol. III - *Real Property,* London: Butterworths 1982 para. 305.

6. G.W. Keeton, *English law: The Judicial Contribution,* Newton Abbot: David and Charles 1974 p. 25.

7. Holdsworth, *ubi sup.* p. 21.

8. Keeton, *ubi sup.* p. 175.

9. Holdsworth, *ubi sup.* p. 25.

10. Stenton, *ubi sup.* p. 643.

11. *Ibid.,* p. 413.

12. P.H. Blair, *Introduction to Anglo-Saxon England,* 2nd Edit. Cambridge: C.U.P. 1977, p. 268.

13. Stenton, *ubi sup.,* p. 648.

14. H.R. Loyn, *Anglo-Saxon England and the Norman Conquest,* 2nd Ed. London: Longman, 1991, p. 332.

15. A.L. Poole, *From Domesday Book to Magna Carta,* 2nd Edit., Oxford: O.U.P. 1955, p. 418.

16. Sir Maurice Powicke, *The Thirteenth Century,* 2nd Edit., Oxford: O.U.P. 1962 p. 34.

17. Poole, *ubi sup.,* p. 418.

18. *Ibid.,* p. 420.

19. *Ibid.,* p. 477.

20. Powicke, *ubi sup.,* p. 29.

21. *Ibid.,* p. 37.

22. *Ibid.*, p. 509.

23. Poole, *ubi sup.*, p. 44 - 45.

24. John Clapham, *A Concise Economic History of Britain,* Cambridge: C.U.P. 1949, pp. 105-110.

26. *Ibid.*, p. 558.

26. *Ibid.*, p. 187.

27. Stenton, *ubi sup.*, p. 644.

28. Powicke, pp. 556-7, where these difficulties are set out in detail.

29. *Ibid.*, p. 558.

30. *Ibid.*, p. 524.

31. *Ibid.*, p. 524.

32. May McKisack, *The Fourteenth Century,* Oxford: 1959, *ubi sup.*, pp. 191-2.

33. *Ibid.*, p. 192.

34. J.D. Mackie, *The Early Tudors,* Oxford: O.U.P., 1952, p. 215.

35. McKisack, *ubi sup.* p. 192.

36. B.E.V. Sabine, *A Short History of Taxation,* London: Butterworths, 1980 p. 58.

37. E.F. Jacob, *The Fifteenth Century,* Oxford: O.U.P., 1961 pp. 333-5.

38. F.C. Dietz, *English Public Finance 1485-1641,* Vol I (1485-1558) 2nd Edn. London: Cass 1964, p. 17.

39. Poole, *ubi sup.* p. 418.

40. *Ibid.*, p. 422 n.

41. McKisack, *ubi sup.*, pp. 154-256.

42. *Ibid.*, p. 223.

43. Jacob, *ubi sup.*, p. 74.

44. *Ibid.*, pp. 74-78.

45. Sabine, *ubi sup.* p. 63.

46. Powicke, *ubi sup.* p. 525.

47. Dietz, *ubi sup.*, Vol. I, pp. 159-160

48. Sabine, *ubi sup.* pp. 74-75.

49. Dietz, *ubi sup.*, Vol. I, p. 161.

50. *Ibid.*, Vol. II (1558-1641), Illinois: Univ. of Illinois, 1921 p. 387.

51. *Ibid.*, p. 387.

52. Mackie, *ubi sup.*, p. 410.

53. Clapham, *ubi sup.*, pp. 286-7.

54. Dietz, *ubi sup.*, Vol. II p. 54.

55. *Ibid.*, p. 393.

56. *Ibid.*, Vol. I, p. 27.

57. Mackie, *ubi sup.*, p. 57.

58. Dietz, *ubi sup.*, Vol. I, p. 25.

59. Clapham, *ubi sup.*, p. 286.

60. Makie, *ubi sup.*, pp. 215-6.

61. *Ibid.*, p. 218.

62. Sabine, *ubi sup.*, p. 70.

63. *Ibid.*, p. 77.

64. Holdsworth, *ubi sup.*, p. 109.

65. Dietz, *ubi sup.*, Vol. I, p. 207.

66. *Ibid.*, Vol. II, pp. 298-9.

67. Sabine, *ubi sup.*, p. 96.

68. Godfrey Davies, *The Early Stuarts*, 2nd Edit., Oxford: O.U.P., 1959, p. 48.

69. J. Coffield, *Popular History of Taxation*, London: Longman, p. 80.

70. Clapham, *ubi sup.*, p. 288.

71. Coffield, *ubi sup.*, p. 76.

72. Clapham, *ubi sup.*, p. 289.

73. Stenton, *ubi sup.*, p. 279.

74. Coffield, *ubi sup.*, p. 80.

75. Sabine, *ubi sup.*, p. 104.

76. *Ibid.*, 101.

77. Holdsworth, *ubi sup.*, p. 104.

78. *Ibid.*, p. 108.

79. J.B. Black *The Reign of Elizabeth*, 2nd Edit, Oxford: O.U.P. 1959, p. 159.

80. Dietz, *ubi sup.*, Vol. I, p. 17.

81. Sabine, *ubi sup.*, p. 147.

82. Holdsworth, *ubi sup.*, p. 3.

83. Halsbury, *ubi sup.*, para. 318, note 4.

84 *Ibid.*

85. Holdsworth, *ubi sup.*, p. 5.

86. Sabine, *ubi sup.*, p. 18.

Also referred to: E. Miller. and J. Hatcher, *Medieval England 1086 to 1348,* London: Longman 1978, p. 44.

PART III

1.   Winston S. Churchill, *The People's Rights*, London: Jonathan Cape, 1909.

2.   *Queensland Hansard*, 3/12/1890.

3.   Reported in W.A. Dowe, *True and False Economics*, n.d., Erskineville, NSW, pp. 137-139.

4.   V.H. Blundell, "Flawed Land Acts 1947-1976", in Nicolaus Tideman (ed.), *Land & Taxation*, London: Shepheard-Walwyn, 1994.

5.   *Second Treatise of Government*, Chap. 9, para. 124.

6.   In an unreported case decided in the 1980s the present writer heard the evidence of a highly respected valuer that a bare site just outside the city of London, in temporary use as a car park, was worth £27$^3/_4$ million. Enquiries of another skilled valuer after the case ended, evoked the reply that the value stated in court was a considerable underestimate.

7.   Liddell and Scott's Greek Dictionary, *sub verbis* quoted.

8.   Maine, *Ancient Law*, pp 134 ff.

9.   Lev. 25: 23.

10. Chief Rabbi Dr J.H. Hertz: *The Pentateuch and Haftorahs*, London: Soncino Press, 1970, 2nd edit. p. 534 (n).

Appendix

1890
A BILL

To declare the Natural Law relating to the Acquisition
and Ownership of Private Property

Preamble

WHEREAS it is essential to the good order of every State
and the welfare of the People, that all persons should have
and enjoy the fruits of their own labour, and to this end it
is expedient to declare the natural laws governing the
acquisition of private property: Be it declared and enacted
by the Queen's Most Excellent Majesty, by and with the
advice and consent of the Legislative Council and
Legislative Assembly of Queensland in Parliament
assembled, and by the authority of the same, as follows:-

Definitions.

"Land"

1. The term "land" means land in its natural condition
resulting from the operation of natural forces unaided and
undirected by man, and does not include any improvements
made upon it.

"Value" of land

2. When the term "value" is used with reference to,
land, it signifies the extent of the difference between the
advantage of having the use of the land in question and the
advantage of having the use of the nearest other land the
use of which can be obtained by mere occupation without
making payment to any person for such use.

"Rent."

3. The return or payment demanded by persons having,

by positive law, the right to the exclusive possession of land, for the permission to use that land, is called "rent."

Rent is therefore a measure of the value of land.

"Labour."

4. The term "labour" includes all modes of exercise of the human faculties, whether of mind or body. It therefore includes the function of supervision or organisation of other labour.

"Wages."

5. The immediate remuneration of labour is called "wages."

"Property."

6. The term "property" includes all forms of material things in the possession of man which have a value for the purpose of exchange or use. It also includes inventions and other immaterial results of the exercise of the faculties of the mind.

"Production."

7. The term "production" includes any act or series of acts by which labour is applied, either directly or indirectly, to property, and the result of which is new property, or property in an altered form, or in a different place.

It also includes the exercise of the faculties of the mind or body, the result of which is property, although the exercise of those faculties was not applied to property.

"Capital."

8. The term "capital" means and includes all forms of property not being land which are in use for the purposes of production. It therefore includes as well property which is consumed or destroyed as property which is not consumed or destroyed in the process of production.

"Interest."

9. The term "interest" is used to denote either the immediate return derived from the use of capital for the purpose of production, or the payment received by the owner of capital from another person by way of return for the use of that capital.

Interest is therefore a measure of the value of the use of capital.

"Productive labour."

10. The term "productive labour" means labour applied for the purpose of producing some property which is, or is intended to be, of greater value than the value of the property (if any) to which the labour is applied.

"Net products."

11. The terms "net products of labour" and "net products" mean the net increase in property resulting from productive labour, after allowing for the cost of production.

"Cost of production."

12. The cost of production may include all or any of the following elements

(1) The replacement of the property which is consumed, or destroyed, or altered in form, or changed in place, in the course of the process of production;

(2) The wages of the labour engaged in the production;

(3) Interest on the capital used in the production

(4) Rent of the land used for the purposes of the production;

(5) Incidental expenses not falling under any of the foregoing heads.

"Positive law."

13. The term "positive law" includes all written laws enacted by a competent legislative authority.

It also includes all unwritten rules declared by any competent judicial authority to be the law of the State.

First Principles.

Equal right of all persons to life and freedom of opportunity.

14. All persons are, by natural law, equally entitled to the right of life, and to the right of freedom for the exercise of their faculties; and no person has, by natural law, any right superior to the right of any other person in this respect.

Natural forces common property.

15. The right to take advantage of natural forces belongs equally to all members of the community.

Land common property.

16. Land, by natural law, the common property of the community.

Positive law.

17. Positive law is the creation of the State, and may be altered or abrogated by the State from time to time.

Functions of positive law with respect to natural law.

18. The application of the natural law of equality and freedom may be modified by positive law, so far as the common advantage of the community may require, but not further or otherwise.

Private rights to land.

19. The rights of individual persons with respect to land are created by, and their incidents depend upon, positive law.

Property the result of labour.

20. All property, other than land., is the product or result of labour.

Measure of wages.

21. The natural and proper measure of wages is such a sum as is a fair immediate recompense for the labour for which they are paid, having regard to its character and duration; but it can never be taken at a less sum than such as is sufficient to maintain the labourer and his family in a state of health and reasonable comfort.

Ownership of net products.

22. The net products of labour belong to the persons who are concerned in the production.

If one person only is concerned in the production the whole net products belong to him.

If more persons than one are concerned in the production, the net products belong to them, and are divisible amongst them, in proportion to the value of their respective contributions to the production.

Application of labour to property.

23. When labour is not applied directly or indirectly to property, the whole products belong to the labourer.

When labour is applied directly or indirectly to property, the person who is lawfully entitled to the use of that property is deemed to be concerned in the production as well as the labourer.

Rights of possessors of land receiving rent.

24. When for the purposes of production the use of land is required, then the rent (if any) payable for that use is a part of the cost of production.

The person who receives the rent is not, by reason only

of his permission to use the land, concerned in the production, but may otherwise be concerned in it.

He is therefore not entitled, by reason only of such permission, to any share of the net products.

Rights of occupiers.

25. For the purpose of ascertaining the net products of productive labour applied to land, and the persons entitled to share in those products, the land to which the labour is applied is to be considered as if it were capital, and were the property of the person who for the time being is entitled to the possession of it.

The amount of that capital is to be taken to be equal to the value of the land burdened with a perpetual rent equal to the rent (if any) payable by him for the time being.

Ownership of products.

26. The share of net products coming to each person who contributes to the production from which they arise is the property of that person, and may, subject to any positive law, be disposed of by him at his pleasure during his lifetime or by will.

Enforcement of rights to share of products.

27. Any person entitled to a share of the net products of any productive labour may enforce that right by proceedings in an Court of competent jurisdiction.

Duty of State.

28. It is the duty of the State to make provision by positive law for securing the proper distribution of the net products of labour in accordance with the principles hereby declared.

Short Title.

29. This Act may be cited as *"The Elementary Property Law of Queensland."*

Also published by Vindex

THE CHAOS MAKERS

The Butterfly & the Cusp
Prof. Frederic J. Jones

The Coming 'Housing' Crash
Fred Harrison

In this unique compilation of economic data on trends in the value of land and natural resources, Prof. Frederic Jones surveys the long-term prospects for the industrial economy to nail down the elusive explanation for the business cycle.

The author employs a new tool in the social sciences - catastrophe theory - of which he is an acknowledged authority. He addresses the hypothesis that land speculators are at the cutting edge of the economy's booms and busts.

Statistical evidence from the UK, USA, Japan, Australia, New Zealand and Denmark is assembled for the first time in a single volume to enable Prof. Jones to forensically dissect the chaos that destroys people's jobs and causes homelessness. Prof. Jones identifies the key policy that would yield sustainable growth.

In his study, Fred Harrison identifies the timing of the next 'housing' crisis in Britain.

ISBN 1 901647 01 3
PRICE: £7.95 pb